£1

Time to wake up!

Time
to
WAKE
UP!

Evangelical fantasy versus biblical realism

Leith Samuel

EP — **EVANGELICAL PRESS**

EVANGELICAL PRESS
12 Wooler Street, Darlington, Co. Durham, DL1 1RQ, England

British Library Cataloguing in Publication Data available

ISBN 0-85234-296-9

Other books by Leith Samuel
How to share your faith
There is an answer

Printed and bound in Great Britain at the Bath Press, Avon

Contents

Acknowledgements

I would like to place on record my deep appreciation of the patience shown to me by the staff of Evangelical Press and for the help received from them and from Nicholas Gray of Pickering and Inglis, and many others who encouraged me to proceed.

I also wish to express my gratitude to Prebendary Dick Lucas for his willingness to write a brief word of commendation when under enormous pressure after the serious bomb damage to St Helen's, Bishopsgate. How I praise God for all the biblical ministry that has flowed from that place!

Leith Samuel
Frinton-on-Sea

Author's preface

This is one of those paperbacks that would not go away! The ideas set out in the following chapters have been simmering in my mind for a number of years.

I have had three reasons for not putting pen to paper sooner.

Firstly, I have thought that others in the English-speaking evangelical world would be able to deal with the issues much more competently and effectively from the same angle of understanding. So I have been waiting hopefully for someone to say simply, and without an array of quotations from other authors, both for and against, what I have been strongly persuaded needs to be said.

Secondly, I have been so busy travelling and preaching that I have had very little time for writing, and have said to myself, 'Don't worry, you are a preacher, not a writer. And your messages in print may be more off-putting than attractive when presented without the warmth of human presence, and eye-ball to eye-ball encounter.' But I do realize that if that argument were carried too far we would have had no Bibles in the first place!

The third reason is a very poor one, only worthy of quick dismissal! This is the fear of losing friends, of being laughed at and called 'out-of-touch', 'old-fashioned', 'simplistic', 'bigoted', the victim of a 'closed mind', not 'open', 'far too dogmatic', 'unable to see both sides', 'hard-hearted', 'incapable of keeping abreast of modern evangelical thinking and practice'. Coupled with this is the fear of no longer being invited to preach in churches and homes where previously I have greatly enjoyed bringing messages from

God's Word and sensing people's warm response to the exposition and application of Scripture.

Then why write at all, and why write now?

1. To fill an apparent gap. While there may already be paperbacks which similarly deal with all these subjects in one slim volume, my attention has not so far been drawn to them. There still seems to be a gap that needs to be filled for some people who call themselves evangelical Christians, by which I mean born-again people who seek to take the Bible as their final authority for all things related to belief and behaviour, but who have been confused, or at least perplexed, by charming, well-meaning and persuasive teachers whose teaching is grounded on a selection from God's Word, rather than on 'the whole counsel of God'.

2. To proclaim God's truth. I have set out to proclaim God's truth as I have come to understand it after many years of diligent Bible study in which I have counted on the Holy Spirit to help me to understand God's Word. This is not a claim to inspiration, but an attempt to refute the allegation that I lack the illumination of the Holy Spirit, for lack of seeking it, or believing it is necessary! I am seeking to present to the reader what the Bible really says about some current issues affecting evangelicals — issues which seem to me to be of the utmost importance, not only for this generation, but for the generations coming after us, who are listening carefully to what we say.

3. To protect God's people. I would love to protect some of God's people from embarking on an unnecessary and frustrating journey which will only lead them into a cul-de-sac of unfulfilled hopes and unrealized expectations. I am not writing out of pique or jealousy, downgrading certain things simply because I have never experienced what others are claiming to know at first hand. I have had the 'sour grapes' epithet thrown at me more than once, but I am not writing because 'They have got what I have not got, so I will run it down as either wrong or unimportant'! I write out of a passionate concern for biblical truth to be understood properly and applied personally. I write because I have met so many believers who have been made to feel that they are second-class Christians because they have been unable to lay claim to certain experiences, such as speaking in tongues or some amazing experience of supernatural healing.

4. To encourage the disappointed and frustrated. I long to encourage some of God's people who have been moving in circles in which there is so much enthusiasm, so much warmth, so much that is exciting, but where they have personally discovered that much that was promised them at the outset has not in fact been delivered. They may even have been told that it was their fault that someone dear to them was not healed. I would like to help them to recover the sense of being precious to God and of not being total failures as Christians. There is no need for them to feel that they are 'also rans', 'out of the battle', or a hindrance to God's purposes in the church he is building in the last decade of the twentieth century. Their 'lack of experience' is not due to ignorance, lack of teaching, unwillingness to yield, or rebellion against the legitimate authority of some under-shepherd who was prepared to direct their personal lives at every turn of the way. Rather it is that God has preserved them from finding what they do not need to seek. Not that I am advocating complacency. Who that takes Philippians 3 seriously could do that? I would love to encourage such people, as those who have 'not yet arrived', to follow on to know the Lord better and better, and to love God's Word and God's people more and more — including those with whom we do not agree on secondary issues, like the form of church government or the mode of baptism, or whether we are to expect charismatic gifts today.

> And yet I want to love thee Lord,
> O light the flame within my heart,
> And I will love thee more and more
> Until I see thee as thou art.

You may not feel that the answers offered do justice to the questions. 'Let every man be fully persuaded in his own mind' — from all the Scriptures!

1.
Is Scripture enough?

When I was a theological student, the battle raged round the question, 'Is Scripture *inspired*? Has God spoken in it?' Then the focus shifted: 'Is Scripture *infallible*? Were the writers deceived at any point? Are the Scriptures totally trustworthy as to the doctrines they teach? Or will they mislead us?' Later there came another shift: 'Are they *inerrant,* accurate in every detail? Or could they sometimes be wrong about titles, names, places, or natural phenomena?' And now? The issue today is: 'Are they *sufficient?* Or do we also need modern prophecies so that we can know the will of God for the people of God living in the last decade of the twentieth century?'

Our Lord's attitude to Scripture

Our Lord's attitude is of the utmost importance for believers. How did he view the Scriptures?

The Old Testament

For a Jewish boy the Scriptures were, of course, what we know as the Old Testament. He would not have considered the Apocrypha to be part of the Word of God, but only the Law, the Prophets and the Sacred Writings, which included the historical books. David was a prophet (Acts 2:30) and the Psalms of David were a very important part of the Word of God for a Jew.

Right at the start of his ministry in Galilee, the Lord declared plainly his attitude to the Old Testament Scriptures: 'Do not think that I have come to abolish the Law or the Prophets; I have not come to abolish them but to fulfil them' (Matthew 5:17). The next two verses further underline this emphatic endorsement of the Holy Scriptures.

In the second phase of his ministry in Jerusalem, as recorded by the apostle John, he says, 'Do not think I will accuse you before the Father. Your accuser is Moses, on whom your hopes are set. If you believed Moses, you would believe me, for he wrote about me. But since you do not believe what he wrote, how are you going to believe what I say?' (John 5:45-47). Can you imagine what comfort I derived from these words, and how my faith was strengthened by them, when I was told in theological college that there was no writing in the time of Moses? While I was still at the Queen's College, Birmingham (the oldest Anglican theological college in the country), the archaeologists came across a very ancient engraving of a man with an inkhorn, so the theory that there was 'no writing in Moses' day' had to be abandoned. It was good to have such confirmation, but Christ's word was quite sufficient for me. I trust it is for you too!

On a later visit to Jerusalem, when his critics were swarming around him in Solomon's Colonnade, accusing him of blasphemy because he, a mere man in their estimation, claimed to be God, he challenged them: 'Is it not written in your Law, "I have said you are gods"? If he called them "gods", to whom the word of God came — and the Scripture cannot be broken — what about the one whom the Father set apart as his very own and sent into the world? Why then do you accuse me of blasphemy because I said, "I am God's Son"?' (John 10:34-36). Even if the Saviour's reference to 'gods' is a little hard to understand, there is no mistaking the crucial phrase: 'The Scripture cannot be broken.' To him the Scriptures formed a great infallible unity and must not be torn apart or thrown aside.

If anyone asks, 'Can we really trust what Christ says about the Scriptures? Or, indeed, about anything?' we do well to ponder the words recorded by John in chapter 12:47-50 of his Gospel: 'As for the person who hears my words but does not keep them, I do not judge him. For I did not come to judge the world, but to save it. There is a judge for the one who rejects me and does not accept my words; that very word which I spoke will condemn him at the last day. For

I did not speak of my own accord, but the Father who sent me commanded me what to say and how to say it. I know that his command [telling me what to say] leads to eternal life. So whatever I say is just what the Father has told me to say.'

God's own words through his Son

Our Lord confirms his claim to be speaking the words the Father gave him to say in what has been described as his 'great high priestly prayer,' recorded in John 17:6-8, where he prayed: 'I have revealed you to those whom you gave me out of the world. They were yours; you gave them to me and they have obeyed your word. Now they know that everything you have given me comes from you. For I gave them the words you gave me and they accepted them.' He goes on to mention one of the all-important consequences of their accepting his words as the words of God: 'They knew with certainty that I came from you, and they believed that you sent me.' In other words, through his teaching they had come to believe in the incarnation of the Son of God and in his saving mission, even if they faltered at the next hurdle they were to face that very night for fear of what would happen to them physically. We must remember that the Holy Spirit, who gives courage and all else that is needed for living a consistent godly life had not yet taken up residence in their hearts (John 14:17-21).

The Gospels and epistles

There are two more things of great importance to be said. Firstly, our Lord promised the inspiration of the Holy Spirit for the writing of the Gospels when he uttered the words recorded in John 14:23-26: 'If anyone loves me, he will obey my teaching... He who does not love me will not obey my teaching. These words you hear are not my own; they belong to the Father who sent me. All this I have spoken while still with you. But the Counsellor, the Holy Spirit, whom the Father will send in my name, will teach you all things and will remind you of everything I have said to you.'

   Let those words sink in: 'The Counsellor ... will remind you of everything I have said...' As Jews they were used to learning by heart, and they would have had brilliant memories by training. In those days there were no computers to consult — or be confused by!

But he is not leaving them to their memories alone. The Spirit will remind them of everything. So our Gospels will be one hundred per cent reliable! We have a completely trustworthy record of what Christ said and did.

The other great work of the Spirit promised by the Lord Jesus in his upper room discourse was that he would instruct them further and inspire the epistles, continuing the Saviour's teaching for the benefit of all generations of believers till he comes again. Let us hear his words: 'I have much more to say to you, more than you can now bear. But when he, the Spirit of truth, comes, he will guide you into all truth. He will not speak on his own; he will speak only what he hears, and he will tell you what is yet to come. He will bring glory to me [literally, "give me the place of honour"] by taking from what is mine and making it known to you' (John 16:12-14).

What would be the point of reading these assurances if we did not have available the words the Saviour is talking about? When the great cricketing missionary, C. T. Studd, the first English batsman to make a century against the Australians, was told theologians in England were questioning the reliability of the Scriptures, he sent to his correspondent the following lines:

'I may look a fool or mad,' laughs Faith,
But I'm not such a fool as I look;
For I trust in a great infallible God
And his great infallible book.

So much for the attitude of the Saviour himself to the Scriptures of both the Old Testament and the promised New Testament. 'The disciple is not above his master, nor the servant above his Lord.' His attitude is to be mine.

The apostles' view

To the apostles, the Scriptures were the voice of God the Holy Spirit. Listen to Peter, speaking after the ascension when they were considering replacing the traitor: 'Brothers, the Scripture had to be fulfilled which the Holy Spirit spoke long ago through the mouth of David concerning Judas, who served as guide for those who arrested Jesus—he was one of our number and shared in this ministry' (Acts

1:16-17). This reference to the Scriptures as the mouthpiece of God is typical.

It is fascinating to see what place the apostle Peter gives to the writings of his brother apostle Paul: 'Bear in mind that our Lord's patience [in delaying his return in judgement and to take his people home] means salvation, just as our dear brother Paul also wrote to you with the wisdom that God gave him. He writes the same way in all his letters, speaking in them of these matters. His letters contain some things that are hard to understand, which ignorant and unstable people distort, as they do the other Scriptures, to their own destruction' (2 Peter 3:15-16). Notice the significant words, 'the other Scriptures'. Peter is actually putting the writings of his dear brother Paul on the same level as the Old Testament, which to a Jew constituted the Scriptures, the Word of God.

We should not be surprised, therefore, to find Paul making similar claims for his own writings in 1 Corinthians 14:36-38: 'Did the word of God originate with you [Corinthians]? Or are you the only people it has reached? If anybody thinks he is a prophet or spiritually gifted, let him acknowledge that what I am writing to you is the Lord's command. If he ignores this, he himself will be ignored.' How do you view this strong claim? Is it true or false? Paul goes on to say in the next chapter what the heart of his gospel is. It is not that gifted men can do exploits for God and find wonderful self-fulfilment. It is not centred in man at all! It is centred in Christ, the Christ who 'died for our sins, ... was buried, ... was raised on the third day' and 'appeared'. 'This is what we preach, and this is what you believed', in other words, 'what brought you to faith' (1 Corinthians 15:1-11). Why turn from a Christ-centred gospel to a gift-centred one? The heart of the gospel is not 'the wonderful things that have happened to me,' but 'the terrible thing that happened to him,' — crucifixion *before* the resurrection.

A historical perspective

The early Church Fathers — the patristic period

When we read the writings of the early Church Fathers, we find ourselves echoing the words of Paul to the Galatians: 'I am astonished that you are so quickly deserting the one who called you by the

grace of Christ and are turning to a different gospel—which is really
no gospel at all' (Galatians 1:6). Whereas the apostles and their
disciples were guided by Scripture, the church leaders who followed
after them were powerfully influenced by the religious climate in
which they found themselves.

Tradition and mystery abounded. One of the traditions in the
mystery religions prominent in Asia at the time was that baptism in
the name of a deity produced a new life. The seeds of the doctrine
of baptismal regeneration were all over the place! Once the element
of mystery was acknowledged in one of the Christian ordinances, it
was only a short step to introducing it to the other one. So miraculous
ceremonies took the place of preaching for personal repentance and
faith in our Lord Jesus Christ as Saviour and Lord, and tradition,
which our Lord had so strongly denounced in favour of Scripture,
began to hold the floor.

In Mark 7:3-9 we read of our Lord's rejection of what had been
added to Scripture without the sanction of the God of those Scriptures. The truth handed down to us, the God-given 'tradition', has
been enshrined for ever in the Holy Scriptures, the apostolic truth.
But it was not long before legends about the apostles, how they were
supposed to have handled the liturgy and conducted worship, how
they interpreted the Bible and unwritten teachings, said to have
come down openly or secretly from them, were being brought
before congregations as 'all part of the Christian faith'. The church
of the Middle Ages hardly knew anything about the Scriptures. They
were hidden behind a maze of superstition and religious tradition.
Small wonder that men like Luther and Zwingli found it so hard to
know God's way of salvation. It was the rediscovery of the Bible
that let the light into their darkened minds and hearts.

Montanism — the 'new voice of the Holy Spirit'

Superstition and tradition were not the only problems facing believers, of whom there have always been a true remnant. There were the
extravagant claims made by Montanus and his followers. Montanus
was a new convert to Christianity in Phrygia, which is in modern
Turkey. He came to believe he was God's new prophet in the middle
of the second century. He proclaimed the new Jerusalem was just
about to descend from heaven. The signal for this was to be a new
outpouring of the Holy Spirit, marked by fresh prophecies, 'words
from the Lord'. The followers of Montanus were encouraged to look

on themselves as the cream of Christians, undergoing preparation for the coming of the Lord as their heavenly Bridegroom. They must expect persecution as part of the purifying process that was to fit them to be his bride people. The movement was driven underground by the official church leaders, surviving for a long time as a protest against formalism and conformity to this world. The famous Tertullian was for a while a Montanist after embracing 'the new prophecy', but left Montanism to found 'Tertullianism'.

The equivalent of Montanism has appeared on the church scene at varying intervals since. It always takes the form of: 'Scripture is not enough. We need direct words from heaven in our day.' The 'enthusiasts' of Calvin's day claimed that the Holy Spirit was inspiring their teachers. They had gone beyond the Scriptures. The will of God was now being revealed through their prophets. and their claims were to be authenticated by 'speaking in tongues'.

Reformation statements about Scripture

Whereas Rome placed the church above the Scriptures, claiming that the church had given the Scriptures to the church and therefore was more fundamental to the welfare of all believers, the Church of England disagreed. This was not just for the sake of Henry VIII's divorce, but because so many of her Reformed scholars could now see that the Scriptures were meant, in the sovereign purposes of God, to be the final authority in all matters of faith and conduct. In the fifth of her Forty-Two Articles (the sixth of the Thirty-Nine) the Church of England made the canonical Scriptures (i.e. the sixty-six recognized books) the ultimate judge of whatever is to be presented to people as necessary for salvation.

In 1559 the French Confession regarded the canonical books as a sure rule of faith, not so much from the consent of the church as from the testimony of the Holy Spirit.

In 1580 the Scottish Confession declared the canonical books to contain the written Word of God. Most evangelicals today would go further and say the Scriptures not only *contain*, but *are*, the Word of God. *Sola Scriptura* is a great watchword!

Roman Catholic Councils

The Council of Trent, held from 1545-1563, was a response to the success of the Protestant movement. The most significant thing for

us here is that Scripture and tradition were declared to have equal
authority, to be equal sources of Christian faith. But it is also
interesting to note that when those attending considered justification by faith, they affirmed that people are inwardly justified not
by faith alone (a key doctrine of the Protestant Reformation) but by
sanctifying grace. In this way a person was made capable of good
works only after his or her co-operation with the divine assistance
offered by grace. The Protestant idea of two sacraments only was
rejected; seven sacraments were affirmed, and these were to be
recognized as conferring grace *ex opere operato,* that is, automati-
cally, whatever the attitude of the person applying for the sacrament.

Vatican I (1869-1870), is famous for the reply of Pope Pius IX
to a dissident bishop: 'Tradition? I am tradition,' and for the
constitution called *Pastor Aeternus* which gave absolute authority
to the pope and promulgated the doctrine of papal infallibility.

Vatican II (1962-1965) had four sessions. The pronouncements
of both Vatican I and Trent were endorsed. There is no turning back
for Rome! 'What I have written I have written,' as Pontius Pilate
said in a different context. The priest's power to offer Christ afresh
in sacrifice was confirmed. In *De Ecclesia* we read that priests are
'given the power of sacred order to offer sacrifice, forgive sin ... and
share at their own level of the ministry, the office of Christ, the sole
mediator'. As at Trent, appeal was made to two sources of divine
revelation: Scripture and tradition. 'Both should be accepted with
equal sentiments of devotion and reverence.' Both of them 'form a
single sacred deposit of the Word of God'. The church is the final
authority, for it is the *magisterium,* or teaching church, that will tell
you what Scripture and tradition mean, and, therefore, what the
faithful have to believe.

Liberalism

Liberalism has abounded in most Protestant churches in Britain for
the last century. The first question the liberal asks when he comes
to the Bible is not: 'What does this mean?' or 'How does this apply
to me today?' Instead he asks, 'Is this true? Can I believe this?'
Many churches have been deserted by the congregations because
they had enough of the preacher sharing his doubts from the pulpit,
instead of his faith!

Barthiansim

Karl Barth, one of the most influential of twentieth-century theologians, reacted strongly against the liberalism of the 1930s. His
commentary on Romans shook the contemporary theological
world. Here was a man who wanted all his readers to recognize the
'otherness' of God. Man is so unholy, so rebellious, and unfitted for
communion with God. God is totally different. He is so holy. Barth
got this from his understanding of Romans. But instead of saying,
'Of course, this is the Word of God. It is bound to be true in our day,
as it will be true for all time,' he came out with the idea that God
could inspire any part of Scripture, so that any portion or verse of
Scripture could *become* the Word of God to the reader. By itself it
is just black print on white paper, but it can become the Word of God
under the dynamic inspiration of the Holy Spirit. Inspiration is not
in the book, but it can get there! Is not this to confuse inspiration with
illumination?

I believe with all my heart in the inspiration of the Scriptures. They
are inspired, whether I read them or not. They are the seed of eternal life.
They are the trysting place where the believer meets his or her Lord
daily. But we need to pray constantly for illumination, bearing in mind
that God has still fresh light to break forth from his holy Word, as the
chaplain to the Pilgrim Fathers said so memorably.

Dr Fisher, who later became Archbishop of Canterbury, once
asked me in his Chester study, 'Do you believe that all the Bible is
equally inspired?' I answered, 'Yes, sir, I do!' 'Do you mean to say
you get as much out of Leviticus as you do out of John's Gospel?'
'No, sir, I don't.' The inspiration is the work of the Holy Spirit
performed once for all in the book. The inspiration is constant, but
the self-revelation of God is progressive. The illumination is the
ongoing work of the Holy Spirit in the mind and heart of the
believing reader.

Before we look at what is called 'prophecy' in some Christian
circles today, may I suggest a 'flash-back' to the late sixteenth
century.

The prophesyings of the sixteenth century

The 'religious exercises' called 'prophesyings' originated about
1571. They were based on the direction in 1 Corinthians 14:31: 'You

can all prophesy in turn so that everyone may be instructed and encouraged.' They were usually held on Saturday mornings, to start with once a fortnight, then stepped up to every week.

Strype, the Reformation historian, tells us that 'The practice was taken up in different places ... particularly in Northamptonshire, and allowed by many bishops in their diocese. The ministers of a diocese, at a set time, met together in some church belonging to a market or other large town, and there each in order explained according to their ability some particular portion of Scripture allotted to them before. After all of them had done, a moderator who was one of the most grave, serious and learned among them, made his observations on what the rest had said, and determined the true sense of the place. All this was to be gone through within a limited time!' At Northampton, the time allowed was two hours, the first speaker occupying three quarters of an hour, the second and third a quarter each, and the moderator the rest. The moderator nominated the speakers, the bishop or archdeacon the moderator, and in some dioceses the moderator was the rural dean.

To quote Strype again, 'Great congregations gathered to hear and to learn. By this means ministers were forced to read authors and to consult expositors and commentaries ... considerably profiting themselves in the knowledge of the Scripture.' In the face of a great dearth of preaching and of men competent to preach, these exercises met a pressing need. They exercised a strong Protestant influence, but were open to abuse. Sometimes men more willing than able would push themselves forward. However, the harm done was far outweighed by the good. When Queen Elizabeth was assured by her informants that these exercises were 'seminaries of Puritanism', she succeeded in suppressing the whole movement, starting with the diocese of Norwich in March 1574 and extending her ban to the whole nation in May 1577. Church history might have been very different but for her overruling a protesting Archbishop Grindal, who had been chaplain to Bishop Ridley, then to King Edward VI, before going to Canterbury, 1575-83.

Prophets ancient and modern

I hope I am not being too unkind if I start a discussion on the nature of prophecy with samples of some modern prophecies which have reached my ears.

'The Lord has told us our church is to be trebled by 1980,' was one of the first modern prophecies related by the minister of that church to Keith Weston and myself at a conference for Christian leaders working in university towns. This prophecy was not fulfilled. By that year the church in question was split. Its membership has never been trebled.

'Look at these twelve prophecies. The Lord gave them to me, and they have all been fulfilled,' said a young father to me. They were all of a very personal nature, mostly about himself and the girl who had agreed to marry him very soon after they met for the first time. And now he believed the Lord had told him he was to go to America, and Above Bar Church, Southampton, was going to pay the fare for his new wife and himself. We had no sense that the Lord wished us to do this, and after we had paid his hotel bill (he had no funds), his brother came down and drove him away.

I had been expounding 1 Peter to a church houseparty at Swanwick in Derbyshire. I had drawn attention to the fact that the believers Peter was addressing in the first instance could expect to face limited suffering, but there was unlimited grace to help them in the time of need (see 1 Peter 5:10-11). When I sat down, a woman got up and said, 'You have been listening to my servant. Now listen to me.' And she proceeded to tell us that things could be difficult for us as we returned home (something I had suggested in my exposition, as I sought to apply the teaching as I went along!) but we must not worry; the Lord says, 'I am with you.' This was my first experience of hearing a woman 'prophesy'.

'You must stay here until revival breaks out in England,' said the visiting American preacher. 'It's going to start here,' he added. 'Revival is coming to England in October,' said one of the Kansas 'sons of the prophets'. So John Wimber brought his whole family to England to see revival at first hand for the first time. But there was, alas, no revival — not so much as a whisper of it!

'The Lord has told me I'm going to die next year,' said one who believes he has lost the gift of expounding Scripture and has been given the gift of prophecy instead, but he is still alive several years after that prophecy was made. Evidently the Lord still has work for him to do on earth. Certainly 'the labourers are few', and it would be wonderful indeed if he went back to expounding the Scriptures, something he was really brilliant at!

'I'm sorry, I can't be your best man on Saturday,' said a young man in the West Country to his friend. 'Why not?' asked the bridegroom. 'Because there was a prophecy last night that you and so and so should not get married!' What happened? The best man dropped out, and the marriage went ahead. Three hundred Christian friends came to wish the couple well and pray for them on the Saturday in question, and the marriage is working out splendidly.

At a gathering of 3,000 charismatics in Brighton in July 1991, which included 800 Catholics, 750 Anglicans and others from many different backgrounds, a speaker declared on the last night, 'All of heaven is rejoicing to see the unity you have here tonight.'

What are these prophecies? Those who utter them speak in good faith, believing that they are the mouthpieces of the Lord. But God is not the author of confusion, and what he says always comes true. So what should we believe about those who think they are prophets of God, or at least have occasional 'words' from God which they simply must pass on or they would not be true to their calling? Before I seek to answer that question, let us look at some of the dictionary definitions.

What is a prophet?

Collins Dictionary, considered by many to be the best available in the English language today, defines prophecy as, firstly, 'a message of divine truth revealing God's will', referring to the content of the message, and secondly, 'the act of uttering such a message', referring to the activity. Then the dictionary gives the popular use of the word: 'a prediction, or guess'. Finally, referring to the ability or gift, it can mean, 'the function, activity or charismatic endowment of a prophet'.

A prophet is defined primarily as a person who speaks by divine inspiration, especially one through whom a divinity expresses his will. Then, as the word is used in the secular press, it may mean 'a person who predicts the future', as in the phrase, 'a prophet of doom'. It can also have the sense of a 'spokesperson for a movement or cause'.

That vast tome called the *Shorter English Dictionary* defines prophecy as 'speaking by divine inspiration or in the name of a deity', and a 'prophet' as 'one who speaks for God or any deity as the inspired revealer or interpreter of his will', while 'the prophets' in the plural refer to 'the Old Testament writings'.

How did the Lord use the word 'prophet'?

When we turn back to the Scriptures from the dictionaries, we find the Lord himself used the word 'prophets' to refer to the Old Testament men with only two exceptions. Let me quote these. The first is in Matthew 10:40-41, where he says, 'He who receives you receives me, and he who receives me receives the one who sent me. Anyone who receives a prophet because he is a prophet will receive a prophet's reward, and anyone who receives a righteous man because he is a righteous man will receive a righteous man's reward.' The 'prophet' here is evidently someone chosen and sent by Christ himself to be his personal representative and spokesman. This refers to his ministry. In this context the word 'righteous' would appear to describe the same man's character. This would tie in with our Lord's warning in Matthew 7:15-23: 'Watch out for false prophets... By their fruit you will recognize them.'

The other exceptional reference is in Matthew 23, that most solemn indictment of the religious leaders of our Lord's own days on earth: 'You build tombs for the [Old Testament] prophets,' as if they would have had no part in their murder had they lived in those days (vv. 29-30). 'You snakes! You brood of vipers! How will you escape being condemned to hell?' Then come the significant words of verse 34: 'Therefore I am sending you [New Testament] prophets and wise men and teachers. Some of them you will kill and crucify; others you will flog in your synagogues and pursue from town to town. And so upon you [of this generation, v. 36] will come all the righteous blood that has been shed on earth, from the blood of righteous Abel to the blood of Zechariah son of Berakiah, whom you murdered between the temple and the altar. I tell you the truth, all this will come upon this generation.'

As it is the Lord of truth speaking, we are not surprised to find prophets and wise men and teachers raised up and sent to that generation. And of the first men sent all except John lost their lives for the gospel of the Lord they loved and served. And upon that generation came the terrible judgement of A.D. 70 at the hands of the Roman overlords against whom the Jews of that generation rose up in ill-fated revolt. There can be little doubt that the prophets of that generation were direct recipients of divine information to be passed on to their hearers, information that was not yet available in written form. But the word 'prophet' was carried over into the next generation of church history to identify travelling preachers, as opposed to elders or deacons of local churches. The credentials of such men had to be carefully scrutinized, for there were plenty of false prophets around, only too eager to take advantage of soft-hearted Christians. Neither of these categories, the false or the soft-hearted, are twentieth-century innovations!

It is instructive that our Lord refers to John the Baptist as the last of the line of prophets associated with the Old Testament. He calls him 'a prophet, and more than a prophet', the one sent before the Lord to prepare his ways. Hence, the popular name given to him, the 'forerunner'.

Prophets in Acts

When we come to the Acts of the Apostles, we find the word 'prophet' used thirty times. Twenty-three of these refer to the Old Testament prophets, a number of whom are named, including Joel (2:16), David (2:30), Samuel (3:24; 13:20) and Isaiah (8:28). The fact that 'all the prophets' point forward with unwavering unity to Christ is mentioned in 3:18, where the prophets are regarded as the mouthpieces of the Holy Spirit, as they are in 3:24, 10:43; 13:27 and 28:23.

In his sermon after the healing of the crippled man in Acts 3 Peter refers to the Lord Jesus as the prophet like Moses promised in Deuteronomy 18 and Stephen makes the same identification in 7:37.

The remaining four references to prophets in the Acts are to New Testament prophets. The first of these is in 11:27, where some prophets came from Jerusalem to Antioch. Among them was Agabus, who 'through the Spirit predicted that a severe famine would spread over the entire Roman world'. God told them this and it happened as God had said. They were not false prophets!

'In the church at Antioch there were prophets and teachers: Barnabas ... and Saul' (Acts 13:1). The next verse tells us that while they were worshipping the Lord and fasting, the Holy Spirit said (we are not told how!), 'Set apart for me Barnabas and Saul for the work to which I have called them.' Now as 'God is not a God of disorder, but of peace', we should expect the work to which they were called to be in line with their gifts and their training through the work they had been doing up to then, namely functioning as prophets and teachers. So it is with the keenest of interest that we examine the record in the next two chapters, till they come back to their home base to report on the work that they had done. What are we looking for? Clear indications of what a prophet and teacher in the church at Antioch could be expected to do elsewhere. And what do we find? They majored in two things. All else was subservient to these two aspects of their work.

They *proclaimed* the good news of justice satisfied by the dying of the Lord Jesus, and forgiveness available for all who would repent and put their trust in him. The corollary to this they also proclaimed. There is a Day of Judgement coming (what a prophetic note!) and none who fail to put their trust in Christ as Saviour will be able to escape him on that day. He is the inescapable Christ.

The other great thing they did was to *teach* the converts. They proclaimed in the power of the Holy Spirit; they were Christ's prophets. And they taught and ordained elders; they were Christ's teachers. 'Sent on their way by the Holy Spirit, ... they proclaimed the word of God in the Jewish synagogues' (Acts 13:4-5).

In Paphos, the capital of Cyprus, the proconsul wanted to hear the Word of God, but the local sorcerer tried to turn him from the faith (vv. 6-8). At this point we find a new element in Paul's ministry as a prophet. He rebukes Elymas as a 'child of the devil and an enemy of everything that is right', and announces publicly that he is going to be blind for a while. And he was immediately struck with blindness! Paul was no false prophet. As far as I know, this element of instant judgement is not to be found among any of those who claim to be God's prophets today!

Apart from another reference to the predictive element in the ministry of a New Testament prophet (21:10), which Paul did not allow to divert him from his plans, the only other reference to the activity of New Testament prophets is in 15:32, where we read that 'Judas and Silas, who themselves were prophets, said much to encourage and strengthen the brothers' wherever they went with the findings of the Council of Jerusalem.

This ties in perfectly with the description of what someone with the gift of prophecy could be expected to do, according to 1 Corinthians 14:1-4: 'Follow the way of love and eagerly desire spiritual gifts, especially the gift of prophecy. For anyone who speaks in a tongue does not speak to men but to God. Indeed, no one understands him; he utters mysteries with his spirit. But [and what an important 'but' this is!] everyone who prophesies speaks to men for their strengthening, encouragement and comfort ... he who prophesies edifies the church.' Prophesying is speaking 'intelligible words with your tongue' (v. 9).

A literal translation of 1 Corinthians 14:18 is 'I thank God speaking in more languages than all of you.' It is not necessary to believe that Paul was claiming to speak in 'unknown tongues' or 'tongues of angels' more than anybody else! See what he then goes on to say: 'But in the church I would rather speak five intelligible words to instruct others than ten thousand words in a tongue' (i.e. a language that they do not understand, whether a natural language or a supernatural one). The odds for Paul are 2,000 – 1 against unintelligible utterance! Should not all who believe Paul is a teacher inspired by God take this very seriously, especially when his very next words are, 'Brothers, stop thinking like children ... in your thinking be adults'? In other words, don't think the noisiest gifts are the most powerful or useful ones. Children love noise, and love to try to prove who is best!

'I would like every one of you to speak in tongues' (v. 5) can with perfect accuracy be translated: 'I would like every one of you to speak in other languages,' which is how I understand it. But whichever way we look at 'tongues', Paul's next phrase is of the utmost importance: 'I would rather have you prophesy.' In other words, he is feeling like Moses when he said, 'Would to God that all the Lord's servants were prophets!' — eager to pass on the great truths which God has revealed.

Is the Bible God's Word for yesterday?

'But the Bible is to me God's word for yesterday. I don't want to hear God's word for yesterday. I want to hear God's word for today,' say some. Others modify it by saying, 'Everything that is said as a modern prophecy must be checked by Scripture.' Do we in fact need modern 'prophecies' in order to know God's will for today?

The biblical evidence

A young lady working for the BBC wrote asking for the Bible verses which indicate that the Scriptures are not only *inspired* in their origin (so that what Scripture says, God says); not only *infallible* in their teaching (not deceived, and not deceiving); not only *inerrant* in their detail (so that titles, places, etc. are accurate), but also *sufficient* to guide the child of God without any additional 'words of the Lord' purporting to be God's special word for today's Christians.

We suggested she looked up 2 Timothy 1:8-14. Paul exhorts young Timothy in verse 8 to join with him 'in suffering for the gospel, by the power of God, who has saved us and called us to a holy life — not because of anything we have done but because of his own purpose and grace. This grace was given us in Christ Jesus before the beginning of time, but it has now been revealed through the appearing of our Saviour, Christ Jesus, who has destroyed death ["Where, O death, is your sting?" 1 Corinthians 15:55] and has brought life and immortality to light through the gospel. And [it was] of this gospel I was appointed a herald [to proclaim it] and an apostle [to be sent to the Gentiles with it, see Galatians 2] and a teacher [to instruct those who respond with faith to it].

'That is why I am suffering as I am. Yet I am not ashamed, because I know whom I have believed, and am convinced that he is able to guard what I have entrusted to him for that day.' That is probably one of the best-loved passages of Scripture, but we need to note that the teaching of the inspired apostle does not stop at these comforting words. He goes on, 'What you heard from me, *keep* as the *pattern of sound teaching,* with faith and love in Christ Jesus.'

He does not look on the teaching he has given to his young friend and colleague in the gospel as *almost* sufficient. The teaching he has already given, and is rounding off in this his last letter, contains all the truth Timothy needs to know, not only for his own spiritual welfare, but for those he is going to teach after Paul has gone to glory. At the time of Paul's writing (around A.D. 63) John's letters have still to come, and John's Gospel too, and his amazing book at the end of our Bibles. All these will be part of the Holy Scriptures. But there will be no new doctrine to take the church or its leaders by surprise or to be added to the essentials of the faith that is in Christ Jesus. Everything we need is in the Scriptures of the Old and New Testaments.

The young lady who wrote was helped by Jude's reference to the faith once for all entrusted to the saints (Jude 3), and 2 Timothy 1:14: 'Guard the good deposit [the essentials of the faith, passed on in God-given words] that was entrusted to you — guard it with the help

of the Holy Spirit who lives in us.' Apostolic teaching is embraced
and passed on as a sacred trust with appropriate help from heaven.

But what helped her most of all was the tail end of 2 Timothy 3:
'Continue in what you have learned and have become convinced of,
because you know those from whom you learned it, and how from
infancy you have known the Holy Scriptures, which are able to make
you wise for salvation through faith in Christ Jesus. All Scripture is
God-breathed and is useful for teaching, rebuking, correcting and
training in righteousness, so that the man of God may be thoroughly
equipped for every good work.'

This last verse assured her that she only needed the Scriptures
in order to reach the maturity she was seeking in faith and love and
service. With the Word of God in her hand and the Spirit of God in
her heart, she could face the future without any sense of being
inadequately provided for or guided because she was not moving in
the circles where modern prophecies are directed to the hearers.
God's Word is enough. And those who listen to the modern
prophecies tend to relegate the Scripture to a secondary position as
a check on whether the one prophesying has said anything
unscriptural. The 'hot-line from heaven' has great attraction!

The true place of Scripture

William Hoste wrote (around 1906, just after theWelsh revival of
1904/5), 'It is quite erroneous to assert that the church gave us the
New Testament Scriptures. She received them. She had in her midst
men of inspired gift, *apostles and prophets* through whom the new
order of things was graciously unfolded, first orally, in what was
called "the apostles' doctrine" (Acts 2:42), afterwards in writing (2
Timothy 1:13-14; 2:1,2,15; 3:15-17) until the complete canon of the
New Testament was built up — Matthew to Revelation. The apostle
Peter classes the contribution made by his brother apostle Paul to
these authoritative written documents "with the other Scriptures".
For the Lord on earth the Old Testament Scriptures were the
infallible, authoritative Word of God. The records he had helped to
inspire as God the Son before he became incarnate he sought to fulfil
as God's servant and their servant in the days of his flesh (e.g.
Matthew 26:50-56). In 1 Timothy 5:18 the inspired apostle Paul
quotes a verse from Luke in the same breath, and as bearing the same

authority, as a verse from Deuteronomy, part of God's Word through Moses. While still at Oxford Dr (later Cardinal) Newman discovered to his surprise after searching the early Church Fathers for support for his High Church views, that "They insist on the Scriptures as the rule of faith, even in proving the most subtle points of the doctrines of the incarnation."'

He goes on, 'The more I read of Athanasius and the rest, the more I see that ancients did make the Scriptures the basis of their belief... I believe it would be extremely difficult to show that tradition is even considered by them "more than interpretive of Scripture". The Fathers do appeal in their controversies to Scripture as a final authority, When this occurs once only it may be an accident. When it occurs again and again uniformly it does invest Scripture with the character of an exclusion rule of faith.' For 'tradition' we may read 'prophecy'.

Nearly 100 years ago, in his book, *Bishops, Priests and Deacons,* William Hoste asked the question, 'What is the character of present-day ministry?' He writes, 'The Spirit of God does not inspire the servant of God today. Inspiration is quite a distinct thing from "the ability God gives" (1 Peter 4:11). Apostles and prophets receive direct revelations from God. Now the canon of Scripture is closed (see Rev. 22) and apostles and prophets exist no longer (except in the printed record of their teaching in our New Testaments), but no exhorter or preacher can truly claim to be inspired. The Spirit brings to our remembrance whatever the Lord has said to us through his Word; something we have meditated on; something that has fed our own souls, in them may become a message with freshness and spontaneity of thought to feed and help others.'

Are speakers inspired today? William Hoste suggests that if anyone got up in a Christian church today and announced he had a direct revelation from God, he would have to be listened to, *if at all, with the greatest reserve,* and all he said scrupulously checked by Scripture. The probability is that the word would not prove to be from God at all. 'Behold I am against the prophets, says the Lord, who use their tongues and say, "He says" ... I sent them not, nor commanded them... They shall not profit this people at all,' says the Lord' (Jeremiah 23:31-32). The strange thing in what is called "the tongues movement" [now the charismatic movement] is that those who claim to receive these direct revelations by the Spirit do not, as far as one gathers, reveal anything fresh. Their utterances, when interpreted, turn out to be exhortations of a well-known character, as that "The Lord is present; we must listen," or that "The Lord's return is near; we must be ready."'

In other words, modern 'prophecies' are usually well-known truisms, nothing that a man or woman familiar with Scripture could not have said quite easily. There is nothing new. And in most cases Scripture itself expresses the same truths much more powerfully and in ways which are much more worthy of being remembered, quoted and acted on. Could we not expect that if the Spirit of God had a special testimony for his children in these last days, and was conveying his messages by tongues and prophecy, 'He would have some fresh and weighty message to convey'?

We cannot do better than respond to Paul's exhortation to Tmothy: 'Until I come, devote yourself to the public reading of Scripture, to preaching and to teaching' (1 Timothy 4:13). Why? Because the Scriptures are not only totally trustworthy, both in matters of doctrine and of historical and geographical detail, but are also sufficient so that through them 'the man of God may be thoroughly equipped for every good work'.

We need faithful Bible teachers. We need urgent biblical exhorters. We need evangelists who are on the wavelength of modern man, but we do not need men who claim to be twentieth-century prophets, raised (so they claim) to proclaim truths received direct from heaven rather than through the Scriptures (2 Timothy 3:15-17). Let us preach the Word. Let us pray for such preachers. Let us listen carefully, prayerfully, expectantly to their preaching.

2.
What is the heart of the gospel?

A well-known evangelical preacher said in my hearing some years ago that the great problem for Martin Luther's generation was guilt, which led to a feeling of total unfitness for the presence of God. So a clear understanding of the cross of Christ was essential for that generation. Consequently it was central in Luther's gospel. God's grace was to be seen at Calvary, shining brilliantly. But today's men, the preacher went on, are not troubled by a sense of guilt. Their problem is powerlessness. So, he reasoned, the heart of the gospel as preached today should not be forgiveness, an apparent irrelevance today, but power — power for living. We live in a power-hungry generation. Let us meet them where they are. So, according to the preacher, the centre of gravity for evangelical preachers needed to be shifted from the cross of Christ to the outpouring of his Holy Spirit on the Day of Pentecost. Here power was to be found. Here was what the modern man needed, and he knew he needed it: power for living, power for service, power for real personal fulfilment. The cross was not to be bypassed, but just downgraded in favour of Pentecost.

A similar, if not identical, idea is abroad today in the evangelical world, but its advocates would not root it in the thinking of the man in the street. They would base it on their understanding of the Bible and on the teaching of many charismatic leaders. The cross must not be missed out. Sinful men and women still need to be reconciled to God in his own appointed way. But the cross is to be seen as only an important staging-post on the way to the real throbbing heart of

Christianity. To change the metaphor, the cross is an essential port of call on the route to the all-important final haven, the desired destination of Pentecost, from which all blessings flow. In other words, we must come to Christ for forgiveness and reconciliation. That makes us elementary Christians. But we must press on beyond the cross to the Spirit, and receive his gifts and graces. That makes us first-class Christians.

I am reminded of a thesis by a former Bishop of Salisbury. He and I shared in the closing meeting of a mission to London some years ago. The bishop had announced that his subject would be, 'No Pentecost without Calvary', and I had been looking forward to hearing him opening up the relevant Scriptures, such as John 7:37-39. But when he spoke, he reduced 'Pentecost' to the ability to live the kind of life we have always admired in others and coveted for ourselves. And 'Calvary' was reduced to doing that thing we know we ought to do, but have been shrinking from doing (I think he used the word 'funking') for years. It all had little or nothing to do with Christ. His cross was hidden behind what was supposed to be ours. Our personal experience was to be in the centre of things. The ghastly experience of Christ on the cross was relegated to the background.

If you were asked, 'What is the dominant philosophy of today?' I wonder how you would sum it up. When Professor C. S. Lewis was at Magdalen College, Oxford, he graciously saw me for half an hour, as I had so many messages from the North American continent to pass on to him from grateful readers of his brilliant writings. His humility impressed me. I asked him what serious theological problems he was addressing himself to at the time. He replied, 'The Logical Positivists have riddled some of my analogies, and until I have an answer to them, I won't be writing any more serious theological literature.' So he was busying himself with the Narnia chronicles. The philosophy of the Logical Positivists is known as 'existentialism'. Professor A. J. (Bill) Ayer was its chief champion. The essence of it can be put like this: 'Only what I have experienced personally, or can experience personally, is truth for me.' For example, I have no experience of resurrection, no matter how many funerals I have attended, so the resurrection of the dead, whether Christ's or anybody else's, is an entirely meaningless concept. The rock on which believers in Christ rest their faith is a nonsense to the existentialist, a sample of outworn religious jargon. Only what comes within the parameters of what I can prove, or have proved already, personally is truth. Everything else is unprovable theory, mere dogma. So experience replaces propositional truth. What other people try to tell me is truth is not truth for me unless I can experience it. This is the dominant philosophy of today.

While many may not have noticed it, this modern philosophy has had a profound effect on the teaching of many churches. Eternity has been played down. Preachers have been afraid of being accused of preaching 'pie in the sky when you die'. Great old hymns like 'Holy, holy, holy ...' have gone out of fashion in many churches. Hymns that reflect what I feel, or would like to feel, have elbowed them off the pitch, if not right into the old-fashioned pavilion! More serious still, we are offered a diet of Christianity as the answer to all our modern problems in an experience-centred society, rather than as the answer to our greatest need as our Creator sees it. Our greatest need is reconciliation with a holy God, our final Judge. But to mention a day of judgement is considered to be threatening! Truth needs to be watered down, made more palatable, more meshed in with the thinking of modern man, less threatening!

In many churches and fellowships people are being assured that what they need most is power for living. And this power comes from the Holy Spirit, so the great focal point is switched from Calvary, where our Lord was crucified for rebel sinners, to Pentecost, where power was released for inadequate men and women.

It is also being argued in ever-widening circles that we must do the equivalent of the New Testament works of power, the signs and wonders produced by Christ and his apostles, because people are word-deaf and cannot be brought to faith by words only (that is the 'cerebral' approach, and it won't work today!), but they are not blind, and if they see us doing miraculous things in the name of Christ, they can be expected to turn to him in great numbers.

But while it is being argued by some with great personal charm that this power preaching speaks to modern man just where he is, we need to ask two questions: Firstly, is this the pattern of preaching we find in the New Testament? Did Paul preach a 'power evangelism'? Did he teach this as the way for other preachers to follow? Did the apostles major in offering power for living through Pentecost? Or did they concentrate on offering pardon for failure and rebellious-ness through the cross of our Lord Jesus Christ? Secondly, does the offer of power produce better or more godly disciples than the offer of pardon and peace through the blood of Christ's cross? The first question is of paramount importance. The second is more pragmatic and not so easy to evaluate, but some attempt must be made to answer it.

The thin red line and the thin green line

A thin red line ran through all the rope belonging to the navy for many generations. It made it difficult for anybody to misappropriate any of it. It has often been said that there is a thin red line running right through the whole Bible, pointing to the redemption which is in Christ Jesus, through his atoning death.

There is also what might be described as 'a thin green line' running through the Scriptures, in all the allusions to the Holy Spirit. This begins with Genesis 1:2, where we read, 'The Spirit of God was hovering over the waters.' The Holy Spirit, not just God's creative breath, but the Third Person of the Trinity, was active in creation. Some people seem to have the idea that the Holy Spirit only began his great activities on the Day of Pentecost, whereas he was deeply involved in mighty works right from the beginning of creation.

A careful working through all the references to the Holy Spirit in the Bible can be most illuminating. Let us consider some of them. We find him brooding over the shapeless deep at creation. In Old Testament times he came in mighty power on a limited number of men enabling them to do great exploits. He illuminated the minds of certain chosen men (known as prophets) so that they received truth from God — truth both for their own times and for coming days. It was he who overshadowed the Virgin Mary, leading to the virgin birth of our Lord and Saviour Jesus Christ. His outpouring of enabling strength (the real meaning of *'dunamis'* in Acts 1:8) on the 120 in the upper room in Jerusalem on the Day of Pentecost, caused them to speak in languages new to them, telling the crowds the wonderful things God had done in and through Christ. It was he who inspired the four Gospel records, and the very first church history book, the Acts of the Apostles, as well as the instruction found in the epistles of Paul, Peter, John and James, not forgetting that fascinating book known as Revelation, or the Apocalypse. He continues to illuminate those Scriptures to individual readers and hearers, and brings about the total transformation of lives through the miracle of regeneration, as he, the Spirit of God, takes the Word of God and makes a child of God. He raises up and directs leaders for God's people, and it is by his activity that they are gifted, instructed, disciplined and anointed for their God-given ministry. His greatest work of all can be summed up in the words the Saviour spoke about him: 'When he is come, he will glorify me', that is, he will 'give me the place of honour', (the basic meaning of the Greek word *doxazo*). Christ did not come, in the economy of God, to give the Holy Spirit the place of honour; the Holy Spirit has come to give the Lord Jesus the place of honour.

So we should not be surprised that while the 'thin green line' is both instructive and impressive, 'the thin red line', the theme of the redemption that is in Christ Jesus, is marvellous and overwhelming.

The first trace of 'the thin red line' is in Genesis 3:15. This is what theologians call the *protevangelium,* the first hint of the gospel: 'He [the seed of the woman] will crush your head, and you [the serpent] will strike his heel.' In the same chapter we read of Adam and Eve covering themselves with fig leaves, and God replacing the covering with the skin of an animal. Here we have another hint of the need for a sacrifice if sin is to be covered.

In Genesis 4 we read of Abel bringing fat portions from some of the first-born of his flock, and finding his offering acceptable to God, whereas Cain brings his harvest offering from the fields he has been working in, only to find his offering unacceptable to God. Small wonder that the writer to the Hebrews picks up this point for the reader's instruction. We see the thin red line once more!

Genesis 22, where Abraham is called on to offer up Isaac on Mount Moriah, gives us a further picture. What God did not ultimately require of Abraham, he did himself: he sacrificed his only Son.

In Exodus 12 - 14 we read the exciting story of the escape from bondage in Egypt. The ground of safety for the Israelites was the slaying of the Passover lamb and the application of its blood to the doorposts, followed by feeding on the lamb. What a picture of the Lamb of God who takes away the sin of the world! A converted Jew, Mark Kagan, has often told how he took a pot of red paint and splashed some on to the door of an outhouse in his backyard, at home and what a beating he got for the red cross he inadvertently produced on that door! The impression that red cross made on his mind was indelible!

Then there is the whole sacrificial system described in Leviticus.

No one sacrifice or offering was adequate on its own to foreshadow in full detail the infinitely great sacrifice of the Lord Jesus. All were needed to present one aspect or another of his redeeming sacrifice. The sacrifices offered in the tabernacle in the wilderness, and years later in Solomon's temple in Jerusalem, all pointed forward to the one perfect and sufficient sacrifice to be made by the Son of God, the King who was born to die.

Psalm 22, that great psalm of suffering which precedes the 'Shepherd Psalm', was obviously in our Lord's mind as he hung upon the cross and uttered its opening words: 'My God, my God, why have you forsaken me?'

The 'Suffering Servant' prophecies, from Isaiah 43 onwards, reaching the great climax of Isaiah 53, all point forward to the Messiah who was to suffer for the sins of his people:

'He was despised and rejected by men,
    a man of sorrows, and familiar with suffering...
Surely he took up our infirmities
    and carried our sorrows,
yet we considered him stricken by God,
    smitten by him, and afflicted.
But he was pierced for our transgressions,
    he was crushed for our iniquities;
the punishment that brought us peace was upon him,
    and by his wounds we are healed.
We all, like sheep, have gone astray,
    each of us has turned to his own way;
and the Lord has laid on him
    the iniquity of us all...
He was led like a lamb to the slaughter
    ... he was taken away ...
For he was cut off from the land of the living;
    for the transgression of my people he was stricken ...
Yet it was the Lord's will to crush him and cause him to suffer,
    ... the Lord makes his life a guilt offering ...
For he bore the sin of many ...'

(Isaiah 53:3-12).

Could any words spell out more clearly an atoning, sub-stitutionary death? No wonder the Ethiopian high official, returning home from Jerusalem reading this marvellous chapter, asks Philip, 'Tell me, please, who is the prophet talking about, himself or someone else?' What a thrill it must have been for Philip, a deacon in the church under siege at Jerusalem (Acts 8:1), to find such an important official from another country reading this very passage of Scripture! Surely Philip was God's man in God's place at God's time when he 'began with that very passage of Scripture and told him the good news about Jesus'. Why not read the whole exciting story afresh for yourself in Acts 8:26-39?

Daniel speaks in his prophecy of the Anointed One, the Messiah, being 'cut off' at a certain time, 'but not for himself' (Daniel 9:26, see NIV footnote).

Zechariah, who prophesied around 520 B.C. says,

'Shout, Daughter of Jerusalem!
See your king comes to you,
    righteous and having salvation,
    gentle and riding on a donkey,
    on a colt, the foal of an donkey'

(Zechariah 9:9).

He also tells us about thirty pieces of silver, the price of a slave, being thrown into the house of the Lord to the potter (Zechariah 11:7-13). How minutely this prophecy was fulfilled! (See Matthew 27:3-10). You can still see the sign pointing the way to that field, very near the spot where Hezekiah's Tunnel ends in the Pool of Siloam.

Why was this shepherd spoken of by Zechariah as riding into Jerusalem? Because 'A fountain will be opened to the house of David and the inhabitants of Jerusalem, to cleanse them from sin and from impurity' (Zechariah 13:1). The fountain was to be opened at great cost to the shepherd, even wounds received in the house of his friends:

'"Awake, O sword, against my shepherd,
    against the man who is close to me!"'
    declares the Lord Almighty.
"Strike the shepherd,
    and the sheep will be scattered ..."'

(Zechariah 13:1-6-7).

So we trace 'the thin red line' through the Old Testament. What of the New Testament?

The centrality of the cross in the New Testament

I will never forget my surprise at hearing Professor Rendle Short of Bristol say that one third of the Gospel records were devoted to the last week of the Saviour's life on earth. When I checked for myself, I found that it is so. Why? Because the death of Christ and the events immediately leading up to and following it constitute the most important event in history. Here sin was dealt with. That outrage to God's holiness was put away by the sacrifice of the Son of God.

There is so much evidence in the New Testament that the cross is the very heart of the Christian faith, taking the death and resurrection of Christ as two parts of the one great truth, that we must be selective rather than exhaustive in our treatment of this.

The Gospels

We shall begin with the angel's words to Joseph: 'Mary ... will give birth to a son, and you are to give him the name Jesus, because he will save his people from their sins' (Matthew 1:21). The way he would save them was to be through his death on the cross.

At Caesarea Philippi, where Peter had made his great confession about the identity of Jesus as Son of God, we read, 'From that time on Jesus began to explain to his disciples that he must go to Jerusalem and suffer many things at the hands of the elders, the chief priests and teachers of the law, and that he must be killed and on the third day be raised to life' (Matthew 16:21). We note the repetition of the word 'must', stressing the inevitability of it.

Not long after, when they were together in Galilee, he said to them, '"The Son of Man is going to be betrayed into the hands of men. They will kill him, and on the third day he will be raised to life." And the disciples were filled with grief' (Matthew 17:22-23). The penny was beginning to drop: he must die.

On another occasion he told them, 'The Son of Man did not come to be served, but to serve, and to give his life as a ransom for many' (Matthew 20:28). 'A ransom', an *antilutron* as the Greek has it, refers to a price paid so that someone, or some person taken captive, may be set free.

We will look at just one more reference from Matthew. At the Passover meal with his disciples, we read, 'Then Jesus took the cup, gave thanks, and offered it to them, saying, "Drink from it, all of you. This is my blood of the covenant which is poured out for many for the forgiveness of sins"' (Matthew 26:27-28). He was not asking them to drink his actual blood. They knew full well that anyone drinking blood would be cut off from the people of God (see Leviticus 3:17; 7:26-27; 17:10-14). 'Any Israelite or any alien living among them who eats any blood — I will set my face against that person who eats blood and will cut him off from his people.' Can you imagine the Lord who imposed that law asking them to incur such an awful penalty?

The cross is central to the Lord's purpose in coming into this world. As Luke says in his Gospel, 'The Son of Man came to seek and to save what was lost' (Luke 19:10). I once heard Professor Karl Barth thunder out to his students in Basle: 'Incarnation without atonement is meaningless.'

When we turn to the Gospel recorded by John we soon come to the words of John the Baptist: '"Look, the Lamb of God, who takes away the sin of the world! ... The reason I came baptizing with water was that he might be revealed to Israel." Then John gave this testimony: "I saw the Spirit come down from heaven as a dove and remain on him. I would not have known him, except that the one who sent me to baptize with water told me, 'The man on whom you see the Spirit come down and remain is he who will baptize with the Holy Spirit.' I have seen and testify that this is the Son of God"' (John 1:29-34).

We come next to those wonderful verses, spoken by the Lord himself, in John 3:14-18: 'Just as Moses lifted up the snake in the desert, so the Son of Man must be lifted up, that everyone who believes in him may have eternal life. For God so loved the world that he gave his one and only Son, that whoever believes in him shall not perish but have eternal life. For God did not send his Son into the world to condemn the world, but to save the world through him. Whoever believes in him is not condemned, but whoever does not believe stands condemned already because he has not believed in the name of God's one and only Son.'

Lifted up was he to die;
'It is finished' was his cry.
Now in heaven exalted high,
Hallelujah! What a Saviour!

In John 8 we read of the Saviour saying to the Pharisees who challenged his claims in the temple courts, 'When you have lifted up the Son of Man, then you will know that I am the one I claim to be.' How would they know? Because his Father was going to raise him from the dead on the third day!

In John 10 the Good Shepherd says, 'I lay down my life for the sheep.' And he assures us that his Father has a special love for him for this very reason: 'I lay down my life — only to take it up again. No one takes it from me, but I lay it down of my own accord. I have authority to lay it down and authority to take it up again. This command [giving this authority] I received from my Father' (John 10:15-18).

When some Greeks expressed the desire to see him at the feast of Passover week, he saw in this the signal for declaring: 'The hour has come for the Son of Man to be glorified.' He goes on to state the great principle he is about to illustrate perfectly: '"Unless a grain of wheat falls to the ground and dies, it remains only a single seed. But if it dies, it produces many seeds. The man who loves his life will lose it, while the man who hates his life in this world will keep it for eternal life... Now my heart is troubled, and what shall I say? 'Father, save me from this hour'? No, it was for this very reason I came to this hour. 'Father, glorify your name!'" Then a voice came from heaven, "I have glorified it, and will glorify it again"' (John 12:23-28).

The death of the Son of God at Calvary is the supreme example of the principle he taught in these verses. While the crowd that heard it was wondering about the voice that they heard, Jesus said, '"This voice was for your benefit, not mine. Now is the time for judgement on this world; now the prince of this world will be driven out. But I, when I am lifted up from the earth, will draw all men to myself [not all men without exception, but all sorts of people from all over the world]." He said this to show the kind of death he was going to die,' that is, what he was about to do at the greatest turning-point of history, the greatest crisis the world has ever known, the issue on which everything will hinge for everybody on the inescapable Day of Judgement. It is true that he draws sinners to himself when he is preached as the only remedy for sin, dying once and for all on a criminal's cross, but that is not what John is saying here.

In John chapter 13 we read of the Lord taking the place of the humblest servant, and washing the feet of the disciples as he got up from the meal table. Peter objects: '"Lord, are you going to wash my feet?" Jesus replied, "You do not realize now what I am doing, but later you will understand." "No," said Peter, "you shall never wash my feet." Jesus answered, "Unless I wash you, you have no part with me." "Then, Lord," Simon Peter replied, "not just my feet but my hands and my head as well!"'

The Lord overrules Peter's protest, and his explanation goes far beyond the immediate situation. He is not just thinking of dusty smelling feet! Jesus answered, 'A person who has had a bath needs only to wash his feet; his whole body is clean ...' The blood he is about to shed is to be the means of their total cleansing, what Paul calls justification by faith. But all of us who have experienced that deep and overall cleansing know only too well that we have to come back to our Saviour every day for the removal of the defilement we have picked up in our daily life in a defiled and rebellious world. Our 'feet' need washing! And back to the cross we must come. The cross is the heart of the Christian faith. 'If we claim to be without sin, we deceive ourselves and the truth is not in us. If we [believers] confess our sins, he is faithful and just and will forgive us our sins and purify us from all unrighteousness' (1 John 1:8-9). 'If we walk in the light,' hiding nothing from him, 'the blood of Jesus Christ, [God's] Son, purifies us [literally, "goes on cleansing us"] from all sin' (1 John 1:7).

The Acts of the Apostles

It might be thought that we only arrive at what the apostles taught and preached when we come to this marvellous short book of early church history, but this is not the case. The Gospels represent very clearly what they taught. The Acts tell us what happened when they brought this teaching before different groups or individuals.

In Acts 2 we read the story of the Day of Pentecost. Spirit-filled men focus on the Lord Jesus, not on the Holy Spirit. There are no less than twenty-four allusions to the Lord Jesus in the outline of the sermon Peter preached on that day, but only three to the Holy Spirit.

This is in perfect accord with the declared intention of the Spirit's coming: 'When he is come, he will give me the place of honour.'

The cross is right at the heart of Peter's preaching: 'You ... put him to death by nailing him to the cross. But God raised him from the dead, freeing him from the agony of death, because it was impossible for death to keep its hold on him.' And all this was 'by God's set purpose and foreknowledge' (Acts 2:23-24). 'You killed the author of life, but God raised him from the dead' (Acts 3:15). 'Jesus Christ of Nazareth, whom you crucified but whom God raised from the dead... Salvation is found in no one else, for there is no other name under heaven given to men by which we must be saved' (Acts 4:10-12) 'The God of our fathers raised Jesus from the dead — whom you had killed by hanging him on a tree. God exalted him to his own right hand as Prince and Saviour that he might give repentance and forgiveness of sins to Israel' (Acts 5:30). Forgiveness of all our sins through the blood Christ shed once for all on that cross is the answer to our greatest need, whoever we are, wherever we live.

It was in Joppa that Peter was prepared by God to use the gospel keys the Lord had entrusted to him to open the door of faith to the Gentiles for the first time. When he reached the house of Cornelius, he was able with good conscience to declare to all the assembled company, '... the message God sent to the people of Israel, telling the good news of peace through Jesus Christ, who is Lord of all... God anointed Jesus of Nazareth with the Holy Spirit and power, and ... he went around doing good and healing all who were under the power of the devil, because God was with him. We are witnesses of everything he did in the country of the Jews and in Jerusalem. They killed him by hanging him on a tree, but God raised him from the dead on the third day and caused him to be seen ... by witnesses whom God had already chosen... He commanded us to preach ... that he is the one whom God appointed as judge of the living and the dead. All the prophets testify about him that everyone who believes in him receives forgiveness of sins through his name.' And what happened? 'While Peter was still speaking these words, the Holy Spirit came on all who heard the message' (Acts 10:36-44). For the Holy Spirit has no greater joy than to bear witness to the faithful preaching of the cross of our Saviour. The cross is the throbbing heart of the Christian faith.

We turn now to Paul's sermon in Antioch of Pisidia. Here we find a Spirit-filled apostle speaking as one of the prophets promised by Christ in Matthew 23:34. He presents to his synagogue audience twenty-six facts about God, twenty-six facts about Christ and focuses especially on the cross, but doesn't mention the Holy Spirit at all! Yet the Holy Spirit was working powerfully in many hearts, and many were added to the Lord that day (Acts 13:16-43).

I have heard it suggested that Paul 'missed the boat' when he preached to the intelligentsia at Athens in Acts 17, because there is no reference to the cross in the outline we have, and that he was aware of his mistake and sought to learn from it when he went to Corinth, which was why he told the Corinthians he was determined to 'know nothing ... except Jesus Christ and him crucified' (1 Corinthians 2:1-5). But if we look at Acts 17:18 we find that Paul was preaching to the Athenians the good news about Jesus and the resurrection. For Paul preaching Jesus involved at least two things: that he was the Messiah for whom the Jews had been waiting for so long (Acts 17:2-3) and that he died for our sins. The leading Athenians would not have been disturbed by either of these ingredients in Paul's message. But when he asserted Christ was risen from the dead, a sample of the resurrection all must face, he was quite orthodox from the Christian point of view, but was heretical in the eyes of the Athenians! Their orthodoxy included the idea that the soul is imprisoned in the body until death brings release. The assertion that the soul would go back into a resurrection body was rank heresy to the Athenians. And the appointment of a day of judgement would hardly be welcome news to them, any more than it is today's bright thinkers! Small wonder that there was such a mixed reaction! But if you go to Athens today, you will find that one of the main streets is called the road of the apostle Paul, and it runs into the road of Dionysius the Areopagite — the only Areopagite commemorated in this way in modern Athens! (See Acts 17:33-34).

Paul surely summarized the whole of his evangelistic ministry in Acts 20:21: 'I have declared to both Jews and Greeks that they must turn to God in repentance and have faith in our Lord Jesus.' When he speaks about completing the task the Lord Jesus has given him, he defines it as 'testifying to the gospel of God's grace' (Acts 20:24). It is Calvary, not Pentecost, which is at the heart of this gospel. Paul underlines this in Acts 26:20-23.

The epistles of Paul

In his great letter to the Romans Paul speaks of the only righteous-ness acknowledged by God: 'This righteousness from God comes through faith in Jesus Christ to all who believe ... and are justified freely by his grace through the redemption that came by Jesus Christ.' How did God do this? Paul goes on to explain: 'God presented him [AV set him forth] as a sacrifice of atonement through faith in his blood' (Romans 3:21-25).

In Romans 4:25 - 5:2 we read that 'Jesus our Lord ... was delivered over to death for our sins and was raised to life for our justification. Therefore ... we have peace with God through our Lord Jesus Christ [let's note the reiteration of the full title and take a leaf out of Paul's book when we speak about him!], through whom we have gained access by faith into this grace [totally undeserved favour] in which we now stand.' The blood of the Son of God was shed on the cross so that sinners might be 'reconciled to [God] through the death of his Son'. If he died to bring us into God's favour, and loves us still, how much more will he keep us in that grace and favour into which he has brought us? (Romans 5:10-11).The cross, not Pentecost, was central in the epistle to the Romans. The first reference to the Holy Spirit is in Romans 5:5 and then he is not referred to again until chapter 8.

This is typical of all Paul's writings. The cross is central in his teaching and thinking. The Holy Spirit has come to give to the Lord Jesus the place of honour. A Spirit-filled preacher cannot make too much of Christ. The Holy Spirit is not jealous of Christ being given this place. He delights in it. So does the Father: 'At the name of Jesus every knee should bow ... and every tongue confess that Jesus Christ is Lord [Jehovah] to the glory [not the envy!] of the God the Father' (Philippians 2:9-11).

Writing to the Corinthians, Paul sums up the gospel by which we are saved, saying, 'Christ died for our sins, ... he was buried ... he was raised on the third day ... and ... appeared to Peter, and then to the Twelve' and other witnesses, including Paul himself. 'This,' says Paul, 'is what we preach, and this is what you believed' (1 Corinthians 15:1-11).

In his very last letter Paul speaks of the Holy Scriptures as being 'able to make you wise for salvation through faith in Christ Jesus' (2 Timothy 3:15-17).

The epistles of Peter

The apostle Peter hardly refers to the Holy Spirit. He is so filled with the Holy Spirit that his writings are full of Christ. Peter tells us that when the Old Testament prophets spoke of the salvation that was to come to the Gentiles through God's grace, the Spirit of Christ who was in them 'predicted the sufferings of Christ and the glories that would follow' (1 Peter 1:10-11). So the Holy Spirit was pointing to Christ then, not drawing attention to himself as being able to take believers further than Christ could; and it is the same Holy Spirit who enables the New Testament preachers to make so much of Christ. No wonder, 'Even angels long to look into these things'!

Think of Peter's glowing description of Christ's work: 'You were redeemed ... with the precious blood of Christ, a lamb without blemish or defect... Through him you believe in God, who raised him from the dead and glorified him, and so your faith and hope are in God' (1 Peter 1:19-21). Or again, 'Christ suffered for you... "He committed no sin, and no deceit was found in his mouth"... He himself bore our sins in his body on the tree, so that we might die to sins and live for righteousness; by his wounds you have been healed' (1 Peter 2:21-24). 'Christ died for sins once for all, the righteous for the unrighteous, to bring you to God' (1 Peter 3:18). So we see, as in his preaching in Acts, here too it is the cross, not Pentecost, which is at the heart of Peter's gospel.

The writings of John

We have already noted earlier John's statement that 'If we walk in the light, ... the blood of Jesus, [God's] Son, purifies us from all sin.' John goes on to say, 'If anybody does sin, we have one who speaks to the Father in our defence — Jesus Christ, the Righteous One. He is the atoning sacrifice for our sins, and not only for ours but also for the sins of the whole world' (1 John 2:1-2). These amazing words are matched by further statements in chapter 3, where we read, 'He appeared so that he might take away our sins. And in him is no sin... The reason the Son of God appeared was to destroy the devil's work' (1 John 3:5,8).

> When Satan tempts me to despair,
> And tells me of the guilt within,

Upward I look, and see him there,
Who made an end of all my sin.

Because my sinless Saviour died
My sinful soul is counted free.
For God the just is satisfied
To look on him, and pardon me.

Once again, we find the cross, not Pentecost, at the heart of the gospel John taught.

The heart of the gospel

There are scores of other verses that could be called as witnesses to the centrality of the cross in the apostolic gospel. It is in the atoning, substitutionary death of our Lord Jesus Christ that the Holy Spirit would have us glory. It is in this great subject that he would have us major (Acts 1:8). For here is the very heart of the Christian faith. The Holy Spirit imparts the enabling strength to proclaim Christ and him crucified. Christ died to sin once. He is not dying today (not even in an 'unbloody manner' as Rome teaches).

When we preach conversion, someone may be converted. When we preach the new birth, someone may be born again. But when we preach the cross, the atoning death of our Lord Jesus, and unbelievers are present, it should be expected that someone present will be convicted of sin and turn to God in repentance and faith, calling upon the name of the Lord Jesus.

The subtle shift from the centrality of God's truth to that of man's experience must be resisted if the church of Jesus Christ is to please God and grow in depth. When we preach Christ crucified, he sees of the travail of his soul and is satisfied, so long as we are honestly desiring to please him, not to build our own little empire.[1] The Holy Spirit has been sent down from heaven to give Christ the glory due to him who loved us unto death. To God our Father and Jesus Christ his Son be all the glory!

Earlier in this chapter I raised two questions which I must now seek to answer. The first was about the evidence for the apostles using, or not using, the methods described in the modern spate of 'power evangelism'. The second was about the effects of this type of evangelism on the personal lives of those involved in it. Does it make them more godly?

Did the apostles use 'power evangelism'?

Only once do we read of the apostles asking for signs and wonders. After the first persecution at the hands of the Jewish hierarchy, following the healing of the lame man at the temple gate, we find them praying, 'Now, Lord, consider their threats and enable your servants to speak your word with great boldness. Stretch out your hand to heal and perform miraculous signs and wonders through the name of your holy servant Jesus.' What happened? 'After they prayed, the place where they were meeting was shaken. And they were all filled with the Holy Spirit and spoke the word of God boldly' (Acts 4:29-31). But we do not read of this phenomenon being repeated. It was a 'one-off' event. The fact that something happens once does not mean it ought always to be so.

Elsewhere we read of Peter's shadow falling on people to their physical benefit, and of multitudes being healed. But we do not find the apostles contriving these situations in order to make inroads with the gospel. This is evident when Peter is to the fore in Acts 1-12, and it is equally apparent when Paul is the leading man of God from Acts 13 onwards. The miracles described were incidental rather than contrived, and are not presented as part of a planned strategy — except as we have seen, in the case of Acts 4:29-31.

What is more, there are contra-indications for the use of such methods. We can read for ourselves that the miracles often attracted persecution rather than great numbers of converts, just as in our Lord's ministry the healing of the cripple at the pool of Bethesda and the raising of Lazarus from the dead both led to increased opposition. Examples of such instances are the healing of the cripple in Acts 3 and the man lame from birth in Acts 14. In the latter case, at first the superstitious crowd wanted to offer sacrifices to Paul and Barnabas, and they had difficulty in preventing them from doing so. Then in the very next verse we read of the crowd being won over by Judaizers from Antioch and Iconium and stoning Paul, dragging him outside the city, thinking he was dead (Acts 14:8-20). If the thesis of power evangelism was right, this should have ended in revival, not stoning!

Does 'power evangelism' make people more godly?

The advocates of power evangelism are among the first to admit that their distinctive approach is not renowned for producing disciples showing signs of greater godliness than ordinary 'straight' evangelicals. 'By their fruit you will recognize them,' said our Lord and Master. The fruit of the Spirit flows from the closeness of our walk with the risen Lord, and does not depend on which theory of evangelism we embrace.

May God give us grace to keep close each day to our Saviour, and to have the joy of seeing more and more sinners turning to him in true repentance and faith, to his praise and everlasting glory. Amen.

1. See Appendix 1: The centrality of the cross

3.
What are the new wineskins?

'God has no more new wine for the old wineskins.' Have you heard this saying? It was very popular among many house-church people not so long ago. The inference was not left to the imagination. The 'old wineskins' were in their eyes the old established churches, such as the Church of England parish churches, Methodist, Baptist, United Reformed, Brethren, Friends (formerly known as Quakers) and the Roman Catholic communion. The independent evangelical churches were not exempt from the strictures that were placed upon all organized so-called 'Christian churches'. All these were representative of the 'old wineskins'. And all Christians inside them must 'come out and join us'. Why? Because the house-church people speaking were fully persuaded that they, and they alone, were in 'God's new thing'. It was along their pipelines that God's full blessing was to flow. So, obviously, anyone wanting God's blessing must join them.

There were exceptions to this rule. I remember asking a well-known house-church leader, 'Do you consider Above Bar Church to be a true church?' He did not hesitate to reply, 'Yes, I do.' But some of his followers in Southampton had made it quite clear to me that they thought Above Bar Church ought to come under their 'apostle'. How often in church history the disciples have gone beyond their teacher! One has only to think of the many 'Calvinists' to whose total teaching John Calvin himself would not have subscribed!

Now the reference to the new wine and the old wineskins goes back to our Lord's own words. Mark records them in chapter 2:22: 'No one pours new wine into old wineskins. If he does, the wine will burst the skins, and both the wine and the wineskins will be ruined. No, he pours new wine into new wineskins.' So runs Peter's inspired report through Mark. Matthew reports the same words in the same context in his chapter 9:17. Luke's research (see Luke 1:1-4) found that the Lord had added another sentence at that time: 'And no one after drinking old wine wants the new, for he says, "The old is better"' (Luke 5:39). Prejudice dies hard. The Lord well knew that Jewish people would not find it easy to forsake traditional Judaism and follow him.

In all three Gospel records the words follow our Lord's reference to the fact that no one who knows anything about materials would dream of patching a torn garment with a piece of unshrunk cloth, or the new piece would pull away from the old, making the tear worse. The context of these statements is significant. People were asking our Lord about the practice of his disciples and they were contrasting their behaviour with that of John the Baptist's disciples and those of the Pharisees. These other men were strictly observing fasts — probably twice a week, every Monday and Thursday, like the Pharisee spoken of in Luke 18.

What did the Lord mean?

What would the Lord's words have meant to his first hearers? It would seem likely that they would have added to the picture painted by John the Baptist when he spoke about the axe being already laid to the root of the tree and continued: 'And every tree that does not produce good fruit will be cut down and thrown into the fire' (Matthew 3:10; Luke 3:9). In other words, the Saviour's teaching cannot be stuck on to the old familiar religion in which they had all been brought up, to patch it up. Something else must be allowed to take its place. God must do a totally 'new thing'.

No one could question that the chief opposition to the Lord came from the religious leaders of his day. The Pharisees and the Sadducees did not see eye to eye with one another, but they were completely united in their opposition to the Lord Jesus. The Pharisees were the formalists. They derived their label from the Hebrew word for 'separate'. They were the largest of the Jewish sects, noted for self-control and long prayers and fussiness about religious rules. On the Sabbath day alone there were 613 rules that had to be kept! Was ever any group of religious people more severely censured than the Pharisees were in Matthew 23? Tradition had come to mean far more to them than Scripture. They had forgotten that men need mercy and forgiveness. 'Do what we tell you and you'll be all right!' Our Lord would have none of this. No wonder they hated him! He would not keep their rules. He exposed what they had added to God's will as revealed in the Scriptures (see, for example, John 5:10-18 and Mark 7:1-19).

The Sadducees were the religious sceptics of their day. They did not believe in angels or demons, or in the resurrection of the dead (Luke 20:27). The soul died with the body. There was nothing after death.

The scribes, or teachers of the law, held an office; they were not a sect. Most of them were Pharisees. They professed to offer instruction without charge or fee, but they had ways of getting their hands on people's money and property (Mark 12:40; Luke 20:47).

These all represented the establishment. They were the old wineskins, the old garment. The new wine — the new life in the Spirit, the new teachings of the Lord Jesus — was not to be attached to the old religion of Judaism to patch it up or bring it up to date in the sight of God. There must be a completely fresh start. Christianity could not be nothing more than an improved Judaism. So what did it involve? Can the new wine vessels be clearly identified in the New Testament? Do they survive today?

Some examples of 'new wineskins'

1. The pulpit replaced the altar as the centre of the worship of the new disciples. Instead of the need to offer a fresh sacrifice of a suitable animal every day, the one full, perfect and sufficient sacrifice of Christ was proclaimed to sinners far and wide. The book of Acts makes clear that the proclamation was not restricted to the pulpit. Wherever people were to be found, there the glorious message of the finished work of Christ was to be proclaimed and explained, and the challenge to trust him as Saviour and obey him as Lord driven home.

So *gospel preaching* replaced the offering of sacrifices and the preacher replaced the priest. The evangelical teacher replaced the Levite serving in the temple. The good news of what Christ had done replaced the good advice about what men had to do. Salvation was to be proclaimed as a free gift, not as a reward for trying to keep rules. Moses had taught salvation by faith in Deuteronomy 30:11-14,19-20 (cf. Romans 10:5-13), but there was a veil over the face of Moses, which prevented the Israelites from seeing the full glory of the gospel. Only when a Jew saw Moses was pointing to Christ for salvation was the veil taken away (2 Corinthians 3:13-18).

2. Christian *baptism* replaced circumcision as the physical sign of membership of the body of God's faithful people. If you go through the Acts of the Apostles you will find that those who believed in the Lord Jesus as the Son of God and the only Saviour were baptized. Christian baptism is a 'new wineskin' for the new wine of the gospel. It did not make people disciples, but it marked them off as such. It presented a beautiful picture of Christ going down into death, being buried and rising again. It symbolized the believer's desire to die with Christ, be buried and live in newness of life, in the power of the Holy Spirit, as he imparts the risen life of Christ. It was also a simple picture of cleansing from sin, even though all the water of the seven oceans could not wash one sin away. Only the blood of Jesus Christ, God's one and only Son, can do that (1 John 1:7-10).

3. *The Lord's Supper* replaced the Passover. Bread and wine on the table replaced the Passover lamb on the altar. The bread did not become the body of Christ, but it pictured it. The wine did not become the blood of Christ, but it represented it. By represented I do not mean re-presented, or offered again. Hebrews 9:25 rules that out. Christ offered himself once and for all upon earth as a sacrifice for sins. He is not offering himself as a sacrifice in heaven. That idea is not to be found in the New Testament, however popular it may be in many so-called 'Christian' circles today. Hebrews 9:24-28; 7:24-28; 10:1-18 rule out very firmly any idea of repetition or re-presentation of the sacrifice of Christ.

Reading the book of Acts, we find that the early Christians, all Jews by birth and upbringing, went on observing the Passover as well as the Lord's Supper. As time went by Good Friday came to be observed instead of the Passover, but the Lord's Supper continues. As Bishop Latimer, the first reformed Bishop of Worcester taught his ministers to say,

Of Christ's body this is a token,
Which on the cross for sins was broken.
Wherefore of your sins you must be forsakers,
If of Christ's life you would be partakers.

We do well to note the word 'token'. Too many seem to be losing sight of this today!

4. Sunday replaced Saturday for worship. This did not happen immediately. From the start the disciples of the Lord Jesus met on *the first day of the week* for Christian teaching and the breaking of bread in remembrance of Christ. The history of the early church members seems to point to the believers worshipping on both the seventh day, as they had previously done as Jews, and on the first day. Then it was on the first day of the week only (see Acts 20:7). Here is another important wineskin, very much with us today, even if not kept holy by many.

5. Written gospel portions in the hand for daily reading replaced the old phylactery system. Go to Jerusalem today and you will find men at the Western Wall with large phylacteries tied round their wrists and foreheads. A tiny portion of God's Word is inside the little box attached by the leather thongs. The boxes on the men praying at the Western Wall today are much bigger than those the archaeologists have unearthed from bygone days. Christians believe *God means his Word to be written on their hearts,* not on their wrists.

6. *Christian psalms or hymns* of Christian experience (as so many of the Old Testament psalms were hymns of David's spiritual experience) and hymns of praise to God and spiritual songs, putting Christian truths to music, have replaced the synagogue order of psalms only, even if it took a long time for Isaac Watts to persuade his father's generation that there was plenty of room in God's purposes for new but biblical words to be written and new tunes to be sung that had never been heard in any synagogue! In these words and tunes new wineskins were to be found for the new wine of the gospel. Many of the new hymns being sung today in evangelical circles are biblically sound in their content. They are extra new wineskins! But some of the words being sung far and wide have a triumphalistic note about them which is foreign to apostolic teaching and impossible to reconcile with it.

7. While the gospel was taken on principle to the synagogues

first ('to the Jew first') it was not long before the early Christians found *they had to meet outside Jewish premises* to worship and teach. The school, or lecture hall, of one Tyrannus is a case in point (Acts 19:9-10). So was the house of Titius Justus, next door to the synagogue in Corinth, where Paul went when the Jews had become abusive, after he had reasoned out of the Scriptures for many Sabbaths, seeking to show that Jesus was the Christ promised in the Old Testament Scriptures.

8. It was not only the buildings that were changed. New titles were given to the leading men in the new buildings or meeting-places. *Deacons* were appointed as well as elders. The synagogue had known elders. It had not known deacons. The *elders* were all different too: they were appointed for their maturity in the Christian faith; they were to care for people, as well as for truth; they were appointed in every church and the qualifications for eldership were not kept hush-hush! (See Acts 14:22-23; 1 Timothy 3; Titus 1).

All these features are to be found in our New Testaments, and they are not difficult to find. The God of the church, who had called the body of Christ into existence, provided generously the new wineskins for the new wine, and in spite of gross apostasy in many so-called Christian churches and in spite of the unfaithfulness of many church leaders, he has kept an unbroken chain, generation after generation, of groups of gospel believers, faithful to the faith once for all delivered to the saints.

At the time of the great sixteenth-century Reformation, the leading Reformers, whose eyes had been opened by a study of the Scriptures and who could see that the church of Rome was in grave error, had to separate from the mainstream church. So the Church of England came into being, with its Thirty-Nine Articles of faith, once considered as binding.

These Reformers were prepared to die rather than to deny their new-found faith; and many of them did. Who that has once heard the words of Bishop Latimer to Bishop Ridley at Oxford on 16 October 1555 can ever forget them? 'Cheer up, Master Ridley, and play the man! We shall this day by God's grace light such a candle in England as shall never be put out!' The candle has often flickered, but by the grace of God it has never been put out. Nor will it be, in spite of Anglican archbishops going to see the pope, cap in hand, in hope of unity with Rome once more!

Marks of a true church

These sixteenth-century Reformers had a simple test for finding out if a church were a true church or not.They looked for three marks: Firstly, was the Word of God being faithfully preached? Secondly, were the sacraments being faithfully administered? That is to say, were they treated not as saving agencies, but as signs that the Lord himself had instituted to point to himself and his finished work on the cross for salvation? Thirdly, was discipline lovingly and faithfully administered? Or was every member free to do what was right in his own eyes?

When we look at churches in Britain and elsewhere today, is it not obvious that, from the standpoint of these three tests, many have lost the right to be known as Christian churches and should therefore cease to function in the name of Christ? But there are ever so many more that are battling on faithfully, seeking to worship God in Spirit and in truth and to make Christ known. He seems to have plenty of wine for these 'old wineskins'. May they flourish more and more through the preaching of God's Word and the praising of his name. Let them go on explaining Scripture and applying it. Our country desperately needs such churches.

It would also be good to see the large house-churches, many of whose members have come to them as former members of other churches where they were not satisfied, also giving their members more and more good solid Bible-teaching. Let us hear less of tongues and more of the Lord, less of 'prophecies' and more of the Scriptures, as so many of them settle into the position of a denomination seeking to be more scriptural than the rest, but no longer saying, 'You must all join us.'

An illustration from Eastern Europe

It was on 21 August 1968 that the Russians moved into Czechoslovakia in great strength in order to crush Dubcek and his brand of 'Communism with a human face'. The churches knew that they would be in for a more difficult time than before. But that event was not going to destroy their hope that one day things would be different, and there would be freedom once again (as there is now) for the preaching of God's good news to all who were willing to listen.

When the Russians drove in, a leading Slovakian scientist was going home with his wife after some months of research at the Institute of Sound and Vibration in the University of Southampton. This man was an elder in the Free Evangelical Church in Bratislava. He had been in our congregation for a year, and reckoned it would be helpful for his group of churches to have the sort of Bible teaching given regularly in Above Bar Church — systematic consecutive exposition of the Scriptures, applied relevantly to the hearers. So in 1969, to the surprise and evident pleasure of the believers, I was given a visa (very few Western preachers were being allowed in at that time) to preach behind what was then the Iron Curtain. At the invitation of the church leaders I have been regularly ever since to preach and teach and have private consultations. It has been most encouraging to see their faithful stand for the truth of the gospel and their courageous use of the opportunities available for them to spread the gospel, with colleagues at work, neighbours, or people with whom they were doing their National Service, to quote a few examples.

When the Communist Revolution took place in 1948, the party bosses said virtually, 'We will allow you to go on meeting in your own buildings. The streets belong to us, so you will not be holding any open-air services. And there will be no religious propaganda at people's front doors. The proletariat (the masses of the people) is ours. The mass media are ours. You will not have access to them. We are tolerating you now, but scientific atheism will have nailed up your coffin in twenty years' time. You will not survive.'

However, it was my privilege to be there twenty years later, and to hear from the elder and his minister that their membership was twice as big as it had been at the time of the revolution! In the past twenty years it has doubled again. What is more, the believers have built a number of very impressive new church buildings, with ample living accommodation so that the pastors are well housed, and there is plenty of accommodation for large conferences. They have done this with their own architects and skilled labourers and their own manual labour. What they didn't know how to do, they quickly learnt, both men and women! Believers in the West were privileged to help a little with the provision of organs, and the cost of some of the more expensive materials.

Attempts had been made on the life of one pastor whom I know well, and several of the elders had been in prison in the early days of the regime for preaching without official permission from the appointed authorities, who were all party members. All but one of those who were in prison for two years looked on that experience as being in one of the best theological colleges open anywhere! They saturated their minds in the Word of God, and came out longing to share with others the truths that had come alive to them in that circumscribed situation. I was deeply impressed by the testimony of these men, but saddened by the thought that the only one who thought God had let him down by permitting this confinement (which did not involve any physical beatings-up) had lost his way with the congregations. No one likes listening to a bitter man!

The danger facing these evangelical churches in those days was the matter of survival. Could they hold out? There was also the question of propagation. Could they actually add to their numbers under such a repressive regime?

Now, in the nineties, a new threat faces them. This time it comes from the West, not from the East, and it comes from people calling themselves Christians, not from atheists. Let me explain.

When I was in Banska Bystryca not long ago I was shown a copy of a booklet being circulated by followers of a German preacher, Horst Schaffranek. He is an ardent advocate of the teaching that God has no more new wine for the old wineskins. In his introduction he says, 'The saints all over the world are divided into about 20,000 denominations ... each considering itself to be an expression of God's will and of biblical truth. Locally and generally, the believers live in separation from one another, according to the tradition of their own denomination or movement.'

He then quotes Arthur Wallis as saying, 'I don't see any future for the denominations, as I cannot find them in God's plan. They are incompatible with his declared purpose for his church in this age.' This booklet proceeds to tell the reader, 'The Lord wants to touch every part of you: your body where it is physically sick' (we will consider the implications of that in the chapter on healing), 'your soul, your disappointment, and the low expectation you have got used to... The Lord wants to wake you up and tell you, "Would you please like to receive a new vision for your life ... of what you could be if only you listened carefully to the Lord?"' (i.e. speaking through us, his charismatically gifted and divinely appointed leaders).

Some readers may wonder why I quote an unknown German preacher when they are not at all likely to come across his propaganda. The answer is simple: Schaffranek is typical of many like him. These men claim that we are breaking the unity of the body of Christ if we do not listen to them and submit to their leadership, for they represent God's 'new thing' for the last decade of the twentieth century. If we listen to them, 'The body of Christ will be effective without any denominational organization.' In other words, you must leave your church, your traditional local church, no matter what its history may be of breaking away from error exposed by the Scriptures, and you must join the new fellowship or community church, or whatever name it goes by in your locality. 'Blessings in the Spirit happen through Spirit-filled brothers and sisters. When you turn to them you will be blessed... If we want to obey the Lord, we have to love the brothers and sisters in our town first.' (Is there anything new about that? Do not those who are truly born again love already all those who are born again because of the same spiritual life indwelling each?) Then comes the punch-line: 'The Holy Spirit is not willing to operate and express himself to full extent within the limited sector of a denomination.' Is not the inference crystal clear? You must all leave your local churches and come under our God-sent leadership, and we will tie you all together. We will succeed where the ecumenical movement has failed!

'The Holy Spirit is looking for people who will obey him and not only the Bible.' There can be no question that these leaders are claiming that God has raised them up to put an end to all denominational leadership for those who want to go God's way. Are we being unfair to them when we say that they seem to be putting the voice of the Holy Spirit speaking through them today above the voice of the Spirit speaking through the Scriptures? If they do that, they are heading down the road that leads to major heresies, and overturning the teaching of Scripture. For Scripture puts the voice of the Spirit speaking through the Scriptures above all other voices. '[Look] to the Law and [hold] to the testimony! If they do not speak according to this word, they have no light of dawn' (Isaiah 8:20). This warning comes in the context of alleged supernatural messages that are very relevant to the hearers (see also 2 Timothy 1:13-14; 2:15; 3:15-17 and 2 Thessalonians 2 :1-3).

Then comes the most serious charge of all, under the heading of 'idolatry'. Believers in the old denominational systems are all apparently in 'self-made Bible systems' and these are idols. So it is nothing less than idolatry to stay in your own church! Now this may well be true of unreformed churches, where the teaching of the Bible is flatly contradicted by the traditions of that church, or liberal churches where the Bible is totally neglected, and modern theological theories hold the whip hand. But it is certainly not true of churches committed to loyal and warm-hearted adherence to the reformed faith. On the other hand, does it not savour of idolatry to put the teaching of these new leaders above the teaching of the Holy Scriptures, which are inspired, infallible, inerrant and sufficient to convey the will of God to all generations of believers until Christ returns in glory and power?

Returning to the booklet, we have on page 9 a fascinating description of the new leaders' willingness to take over all existing churches if only they will repent of their denominationalism and submit to these men: 'The Holy Spirit can act directly through these men who always work in groups [apostles, prophets, evangelists, pastors and teachers] and the flock will be led. If the flock moves on [a favourite phrase with all such leaders] it will not stay for one moment at the same place where it has been.' Progress is guaranteed! The restless search for change is on: there must always be something new! The worship 'programme' must always be different, fresh, imaginative, original. At all costs we must get rid of the old hymn-prayer-hymn-sermon-hymn sandwich!

On page 12 we read that 'The first churches were glorious places of God.' If we think that we must wear rose-tinted spectacles when we read 1 Corinthians, in which there is not a single chapter that is not basically corrective — yes, even chapter 13! And what about Galatians 1 and 3, and Philippians?

On page 14 we are told that 'We have made of the church little boxes with big quality labels on the outside,' and 'The numerous churches are but substitutes ... they hinder God's real intention.'

In other words, the old wineskins have leaked so badly that all the good wine of gospel truth has escaped, and we must turn to the new structure of 'only one church in every city under our leadership'. This is God's new thing, for 'Correct structure is the key to effective evangelism and worship acceptable to God.' This will inevitably mean there being only one church in any given city, and 'Theological teaching becomes correct when the body is put in order.' The process of putting the body in order starts when the leaders gather and bow down to the floor before the Lord together asking, 'Lord, what are we to do? What's the next step?'

Twice a year in Britain a large group of 'apostles and prophets' get together. They meet to wait on the Lord for his latest word, which they then take back to their faithful followers. On one occasion the 'word of the Lord' was: 'Intercession must be corporate, not private.' But what about our Lord's teaching in Matthew 6 about going away from everybody to seek God's face in private?

Whereas the new prophets would say, 'Faithfulness to the fresh word of the Lord through these leaders is the key to fresh blessing,' checking the word by Scripture (as Arthur Wallis once said to me personally), surely the two prerequisites for further blessing are trusting in the Lord with all our hearts, and not leaning to our own natural understanding, combined with faithfulness to God's written Word, the Bible, which is inspired by God, infallible in its teaching, inerrant in every detail and sufficient as the final authority for the church of Jesus Christ till he returns in glory and great power. That is to say, these are the necessary conditions for blessing that lasts, and is not here today and gone tomorrow! Of course, there must not be a slavish dependence on the text of Scripture, as if all that is needed were 'fundamentalism'. There must also be a very real dependence on the Holy Spirit who inspired the Word for the illumination and application of that inspired Word to the hearts and minds of the hearers.

The key page of this powerful piece of special pleading, which I am quoting at length because it is typical of 'new wine' pressure everywhere, is the last in the booklet (page 24). Let me quote: 'The church is the instrument through which God is glorified and reveals himself. [Who could take exception to that?] The Holy Spirit alone builds the church through his specially ordained servants [here he means the new apostles and prophets, presenting the secrets of the 'new wine'], which are authorized and legitimated in a way artificial clerical ministers could never be. If the believers in any city step out of their groups and denominations and start sharing fellowship with all other believers where they live, serving one another and helping one another to be equipped for service, then this becomes a seedling for the one church of Jesus Christ in that city. This church is God's workshop where he wants to act in order to be glorified in front of the world.' Then comes the final appeal: 'If we desire to be people after God's own heart, all our service, all our commitment, all our attention has to focus on the church, its re-establishment and completion.' The key word here is 're-establishment'.

I do not believe there is scriptural evidence that all who trust in Christ for salvation are going to be united in a single structure in every city, under one leadership. God has been pleased to honour the preaching of Christ's gospel in a great variety of church situations and affiliations. While it is our solemn duty, as those under the authority of the Lord who prayed that his people might be one (and this is where the British Evangelical Council is so helpful in contrast with Churches Together), to keep as close to one another as is possible across our local church loyalties, and to test our church structures by Scripture, I see no sufficient reason to 'come out' of an independent evangelical church and submit to the claims of those who call themselves God's new prophets and apostles. Nor do most of my friends in Slovakia.

May we all long to be faithful to Christ and his gospel, and helpful to all his people as we meet them. May we long for his appearing, when all man-made barriers will disappear. Let us come to him every day asking to be filled afresh with this 'new wine'.

4.
What are the 'greater works' of John 14:12?

In his upper room discourse to his disciples on the same night on which he was betrayed, our Lord Jesus said to the eleven that remained after Judas had left them, 'Anyone who has faith in me will do what I have been doing. He will do even greater things than these, bcause I am going to the Father' (John 14:12).

There is a really important question to be faced here: does this promise refer to believers of all generations? If so, it applies to us today, and we should be doing the same works of healing and power that are recorded as being done by the Saviour in New Testament days. Our Christian teachers should be doing them and encouraging us to do them, and we should feel guilty if we are not seeing a measure of lasting success in this direction.

On the other hand, if the promise does not refer to any Christians beyond the immediate small circle of those eleven who heard and reported the words, then we should not feel guilty if we are not doing the sort of things the Saviour did during his three years' ministry in Galilee and Judea. Indeed, if we were to attempt to do such things, or advertise that such an attempt was to be made, we would be raising wrong and unjustifiable expectations which neither we nor those who heard us were able to deliver.

We have to admit that many of the songs being sung today with great gusto in many evangelical circles express or imply or arouse great expectations, as if we should all be doing the great works that marked the Saviour's three-year ministry in Palestine of old. Take, for example, some words from one of Graham Kendrick's very popular songs:

Restore, O Lord, the honour of your name,
In works of sovereign power ,
Come shake the earth again,
That men may see...[1]

The reference to 'works of power' highlights a comparatively new idea imported from the United States, which has had an enormous impact on British evangelical circles. It can be summed up very simply: 'Evangelicals in Britain have been faithfully preaching the gospel with very little fruit to show for it. The main approach has been through words. People don't sit up and take notice. If only the preachers could produce works of power as well, people would be flocking into the places of demonstration and proclamation. There would be abundant fruit to show for the two-edged approach.'

The burning question for us is this: is this true? Is this what the Saviour had in mind when he spoke of 'the works that I do ... ' and said, 'Greater works shall you do'? When we study the Bible, there are three important questions we should always bear in mind: To whom were these words spoken? In what circumstances were they spoken? How were they understood by the first hearers?

To whom were these words spoken?

The answer to this first question is that the words of John 14:12 were spoken to a very select company, namely the eleven apostles who remained with the Saviour in the upper room after Judas had departed to betray him. They were not addressed to the 5,000 whom he fed in Galilee, or to the 4,000 he fed soon after, but only to those to whom he had given power and authority to overcome all demons and to cure diseases in Galilee (Luke 9:1). He did not say anything about 'greater works' to the seventy-two who were appointed to go ahead of him in pairs to every town and place he himself intended to visit, as recorded in Luke 10:1, even though they were commissioned to heal the sick and say, 'The kingdom of God is near you.' It is also significant that in their commission the punch-line was not about watching the miracles but about listening to their words. 'He who listens to you listens to me: he who rejects you rejects me; but he who rejects me rejects the one who sent me' (Luke 10:16). The message, not the miracles, was all-important.

When the seventy-two came back from their mission, bubbling over with the sense of power their successes had given them, the Lord warned them against pride, reminding them of Satan's fall from heaven through pride, and says (and we should note that these words were specifically addressed to the seventy-two), 'I have given you authority... to overcome all the power of the enemy; nothing will harm you. However, do not rejoice that the spirits submit to you, but rejoice that your names are written in heaven.' In other words, our relationship with God is so much more important than anything we can do in his name. Truth revealed to us by the Father, Lord of heaven and earth, is far more important than any service we can do for him. Pride in 'successful service' will be an insurmountable barrier to further usefulness — until we repent of it.

In what circumstances were they spoken?

These words were spoken as part of a briefing given by the Lord on the eve of his death and just prior to the great high priestly prayer recorded in John 17. The men to whom he had given all the words the Father had given him for them were going to need special help if they were to be accepted as the authentic mouthpieces of the risen Lord of life and glory. Our faith, over sixty generations later, hinges on the Holy Spirit working through their words. We are among the millions who have come to believe on the Lord Jesus Christ through their words (John 17:20; 20:30-31). The marks of an apostle must be seen in their ministry (2 Corinthians 12:12). Their works authenticated their words. If every Christian had been able to do these works which the Saviour did, how would it ever have been possible to know who had apostolic authority as a fully authorized teacher of truth for all time? As surely as the Saviour himself was attested, as Peter said on the Day of Pentecost, 'by miracles, wonders and signs, which God did among you through him' — that is, among the Jews of that day, as they themselves knew — so would God attest the ministry of this small body appointed to carry on the revealing to an ignorant world of the truths which Christ had entrusted to them. But we seek in vain for indications that those brought to faith in Christ through their teaching were to be similarly authenticated. The confession of their faith in Christ and the fruit of the Spirit seen in their lives were to be the evidence that they were genuine.

What would these words have meant to the first hearers?

The answer to this question is not difficult to find. Just as they had been able to do remarkable things when they were sent forth with the seventy-two to demonstrate the authenticity of the claims of Jesus to be the long-awaited Messiah and the compassion of a God who cares, so they would be found doing remarkable things after his atoning death and his bodily resurrection and ascension to God's right hand. These works would further demonstrate the validity of his claims, as well as authenticating their own ministry as his apostles, personally authorized representatives who could be counted on to give totally accurate accounts of his teaching.

Matthew, the former tax-gatherer, was inspired to give us a true record of the words he heard the Saviour say. Mark gives us Peter's memories, inspired and safeguarded by the same Holy Spirit, as Papias tells us. Luke was enabled by the Holy Spirit to do a task of brilliant research into many first-hand sources (as he tells us in his prologue or foreword), including what he learned from Mary. John, the beloved disciple, gives us a fuller record of things the Son of God said. How much poorer we would be without this inspired and wonderful record found in what has been the favourite Gospel of so many believers of all generations!

Christ said they would do the works he did, and the New Testament record tells us that they did do so. Did Christ heal a man in Jerusalem who had been a cripple a long time? (John 5). Peter and John did something very similar (Acts 3). Did Christ cast out demons with a word of authority? (Mark 1). The apostles did the same (Acts 5:15-16). Did Christ restore sight to the blind? (John 9). Multitudes that were blind and deaf were healed by the apostles of these infirmities: 'The apostles performed many miraculous signs and wonders among the people... Crowds gathered also from the towns around Jerusalem, bringing their sick and those tormented by evil spirits, and all of them were healed' (Acts 5:12-16). Even Peter's shadow seemed to effect a marvellous healing influence. We

read of a similar effect from handkerchiefs and aprons which had
been in contact with Paul's skin, when 'God did extraordinary
miracles through Paul,' showing his compassion, as well as attesting
Paul's apostleship (Acts 19:11-12). Did Christ raise people from the
dead? Yes indeed. We read of three: Jairus' daughter, the widow of
Nain's son and Lazarus of Bethany. Likewise the apostle Peter
raised Tabitha (or Dorcas) from the dead (Acts 9) and some thirty
years later, Paul, whose apostleship had been questioned by his
critics in Corinth and Galatia, raised Eutychus from the dead (Acts
20).

Their Master did wonderful works, wonders and signs, signs of
his being God's Messiah. He himself drew attention to these signs
when the disciples of John the Baptist asked him, 'Are you the one
who was to come?' ('The coming one' was a code name for Messiah
among the Jews). Similarly, the wonderful works accomplished by
the apostles accredited them as his official, duly authorized representatives, absolutely trustworthy teachers of the truths he taught.

Is it not significant that when James was beheaded at the order
of King Herod Antipas there was no suggestion of replacing him by
a fresh member of the apostolic band as there had been when Judas
committed suicide, leaving a gap in the company that had been so
close to the Lord in his three years' ministry? Their understanding
of Scripture had made it clear to them that Judas was to be replaced,
as Acts 1:21-22 indicates. But there is no such awareness of any
need to replace James. Saul of Tarsus had been added to their select
company by the risen Lord himself. Ananias was in no uncertainty
about Saul seeing the risen Lord (Acts 9:15). The number was now
complete. There are no apostles of this category today. Apostolic
succession consists not in men ordained by men who have had hands
laid upon them in an unbroken chain right back to the apostles. It
consists rather in faithfulness to the truth taught by the apostles. If
some groups of Christians call their top leaders 'apostles' on the
ground that they have planted churches somewhere, and because
they believe the risen Lord goes on giving new apostles to every
generation, that is their prerogative. But they should not be surprised
if those outside their ecclesiastical circles look on these men as
having no leadership authority whatsoever over anybody outside
such groups. The days of authoritative apostles, having authority
over all the churches known as Christian (1 Corinthians 14:33-38)
belong to New Testament times, not to today.

Paul makes mention of the 'things that mark an apostle' in his vindication of his authority over the church at Corinth (2 Corinthians 12:12). It is clear from the way he puts it that there is something quite unmistakable about an apostle: 'I am not in the least inferior to the "super-apostles" ... The things that mark an apostle — signs, wonders and miracles — were done among you with great perseverance.' Is it not evident from this that there were certain things which only an apostle could do? If every Christian could do them in the name of the Lord Jesus Christ, what was the point of Paul's question? Is it not clear from Paul's words in this passsage that there were certain things that only an apostle could do in the name of Christ, things that distinguished him from other Christians, without for a moment questioning the right of the latter to be known as Christians? Since the apostles were commissioned to convey infallible truth, it was important that everybody should know precisely who was authorized by the risen Lord to do this. An apostle was appointed by Christ himself (Mark 3:13-18) and was named as an 'apostle' by Christ, while the rest of his followers were known as 'disciples'. An apostle had to be a witness of the risen Lord (that is why Paul makes this point at the start of his discussion in 1 Corinthians 9), and a recipient of divine revelation from the lips of Christ himself (Mark 3:12; Galatians 1:11-17; Ephesians 3:1-8; 1 Corinthians 15:7-10).

The inspired record in the Acts of the Apostles (not an insignificant title after all!) tells us clearly how the promise made by Christ was fulfilled by the eleven. Apart from rising from the dead, walking on the water and miraculously feeding hungry multitudes, the works that he did they did also. He did remarkable things; they did remarkable things. The remarkable things he did authenticated his right to speak in his Father's name. The remarkable things they did authenticated their right to speak in his name.

I wonder how it is that so much is made of the earlier part of 1 Corinthians 14 in some circles today, while the last few verses seem to be ignored or dismissed as totally irrelevant to today's world, secular or religious. It is an indication of how far the secular thinking in today's world has captured the thinking of so many of today's church leaders that the apostle's divinely inspired teaching is treated as an indication of how much he was a child of his own culture and generation. The biblical teaching is that the apostles were inspired to give to the people of God truth that was valid for all time till Christ comes again. The doctrine of development of truth is embraced and heavily underlined in official Roman Catholic circles, but those who might be called 'Bible Christians', or 'evangelicals', have until fairly recent years looked on the Bible as their final authority for all matters of belief and behaviour. Yet in today's world we find many who would like to be thought of as sound evangelicals murmuring about culture and toeing the lines laid down by people who would not dream of labelling themselves as 'evangelicals'.

Two questions remain to be answered.

Do Christian teachers today need miraculous works to authenticate their ministry?

The first question is whether Christian teachers today need to be authenticated as having a right to exercise a teaching, preaching and pastoral ministry in the name of Christ by doing the same miraculous works that he and his apostles did.

There certainly should be some authentication because the Saviour said of teachers coming in his name, 'By their fruit you will recognize them' (i.e. as genuine). If the true gospel is faithfully preached, and the life of the preacher matches his teaching, in due season God will honour such teaching with fruit that is to be seen and that remains. But is it right to expect God to enable ordinary Christians, or even gifted Christian teachers, to authenticate their claims to be teachers whom God has appointed by doing miracles, performing works of power, signs and wonders? Men like John Wimber have been saying in books such as *Power Evangelism* that ordinary verbal evangelism has left the masses cold in the U.S.A. and Europe, because it was merely the communication of a message in words addressed to people's ears. If only, runs the new idea, we could address people's eyes with signs and wonders, which they simply could not deny were done in the name of the Lord Jesus Christ, they would find it far easier to believe and people would be crowding into our churches.

But while we read with great delight of the Lord doing great works of power and of the apostles doing equally wonderful things in his name, where does the Scripture say that 'God was pleased by the unassailable evidence of people being miraculously healed to save those that are lost'? There is no such statement in the New Testament. What we do read instead is: 'God was pleased by the foolishness of what was preached [i.e. the message of Christ crucified for our sins] to save those who believe.' So we preach Christ crucified (1 Corinthians 1:18-23; cf. 2 Corinthians 4:6) and all whom the Father draws to his Son come to him (John 6:37-44). We can have every confidence that the ministry of God-sent Christian teachers and preachers in the last decade of the twentieth century will be authenticated by sinners being converted, by transformed lives, homes and relationships, 'new creations' as we read in 2 Corinthians 5:15.

What about the 'greater works' Christ spoke of?

This leads us quite naturally to an understanding of the 'greater works' which our Lord spoke about in that discourse in the upper room. What did he mean by 'greater things [AV, works] than these'? Did anything done by the Saviour fall short of perfection? I am sure no believer would have the audacity to make such an assertion. Everything Christ did was perfect. Even the blind man who needed a second touch because he could only see people who looked like trees walking around (Mark 8:22-26) saw everything in perfect focus after that second touch. Why the need for the second touch? Because the Saviour was using this blind man as a visual aid to show how slow his disciples were to see the truths he had just been sharing with them. No one he touched was made 'just a little better'! They were all perfectly healed. Now you cannot have anything more perfect than perfect, so when the Saviour speaks of 'greater works', he cannot possibly be referring to works which are greater in *quality*. You cannot have anything better than perfect. You cannot improve on perfection.

Some who can see the strength of this argument have said, 'What the Saviour meant was "more numerous". Not greater in quality, but greater in *quantity*.' In other words, believers all over the world can be expected to be involved in the performance of more numerous works of effective healing or supernatural control of nature, or more numerous cases of men and women being raised from physical death. However, there is a fatal objection to this line of thinking: the Greeks have a word for 'more numerous' (*pleiona*) and it is not the word used in the inspired record here. The Lord describes the works as *meizona*, which means 'greater' in some way.

If they cannot be greater in quality because all he did was perfect, and he did not mean greater in number because the Greeks have a word for that, then what do we have left? A simple third alternative: greater in *nature*.

This understanding of the word ties in perfectly with Paul's description of his commission from the risen Lord. We read in Acts 26:17-20, 'I am sending you to them to open their eyes and turn them from darkness to light, and from the power of Satan to God, so that they may receive forgiveness of sins and a place among those who are sanctified by faith in me. So then, King Agrippa', Paul continues, 'I was not disobedient to the vision from heaven. First to those in Damascus, then to those in Jerusalem and in all Judea, and to the Gentiles also, I preached that they should repent and turn to God and prove their repentance by their deeds.'

So Paul was sent to open the eyes of the blind. The physically blind? No, the context makes it abundantly clear that it was the spiritually blind. There may have been many physically blind among these, but the healing of the physically blind is not in Paul's remit here. The work he is commissioned to perform is greater because it is a spiritual work, and unlike physical healing, the benefits of it will last for ever and ever.

Christians today may not be expected to perform the great works of Christ and the apostles, but they can share in the 'greater works'. This comes out very clearly in Philip the deacon's successful evangelism of the Ethiopian eunuch, in the example of those 'who were scattered throughout Judea and Samaria' (Acts 8) and in many clear commands to spread the faith, but there is no command to do signs, wonders and miracles.

The man in the next bed to me in hospital was suffering from MS. He had cried in great pain at home, 'O my God! O my God!' Then he thought, 'Hang on, who is my God? Where is he to be found? He came to the conclusion that during an anticipated visit to the nearby general hospital he would find a Gideon Bible in his locker, and through reading it he would be able to find God. Imagine his disappointment when he found there was no Bible in his locker! However, the Gideons brought him a Bible that evening, and he said later, 'The more I read, the more I believed.' He came to saving faith in the Lord Jesus after getting over his first disappointment that what happened to the crippled man at Bethesda was not promised as a repeat performance for him. His first word when I saw him after coming out of hospital was 'Bethesda!'

Of course he would have appreciated a miracle of healing. It would have been simply wonderful for him to be running round like others of his age (then thirty-four, after fifteen years with MS). 'Let's add thirty-six to thirty-four. What does that make it?' 'Curtains,' he replied. 'Let's suppose your legs were healed miraculously at thirty-four (for God is God and he can heal anybody of anything, though he has not committed himself to doing so) and you come to the end of your days without finding the free gift of the forgiveness of all your sins or the free gift of everlasting life, where are you?'

He was silent for a moment. Then he made it clear that it was far more important for him to find God and God's peace than it was to get healing for his legs. By Easter that year he knew he was a forgiven man and God's peace shone out of him. The great work of physical healing, which an apostle could have performed, was denied him, but he experienced the greater work the Saviour had promised.

As Paul puts it, 'If anyone is in Christ, he is a new creation: the old has gone, the new has come! All this is from God ...' (2 Corinthians 5:17). What a miracle! The greatest miracle in the world today is the miracle of regeneration. Someone who has been notoriously selfish no longer thinks of 'Number One' only. He or she begins to live for God and to long to serve others. Why? Because of this great miracle, the miracle of new birth. Because the Saviour has died that this person might be forgiven, given this totally new life and the power to live this life through the Holy Spirit and in fellowship with other believers, and with a first-class, free, non-transferable ticket for heaven thrown in!

The greatest work of all

There is no greater work on earth than the work of bringing a guilty lost sinner into a personal relationship with our holy God. It is the work with the greatest consequences of all and the one that lasts the longest — for ever.

Saul of Tarsus experienced this 'greater work' in his own life during those three days between the blinding light on the road to Damascus and, in a beautiful picture of his spiritual experience, the scales falling away from his eyes.

Augustine of Hippo experienced this 'greater work' when he picked up the letter to the Romans that he had placed on the garden seat in Milan and read, 'Clothe yourself with the Lord Jesus Christ, and do not think about how to gratify the desires of the sinful nature' (Romans 13:14). Quickened by the searching and demanding Word of God, he found the Spirit who had inspired it gave him the strength to obey it. He rose from his knees in that garden a new creature in union with Christ Jesus.

Thomas Bilney experienced the 'greater work' when kneeling in his room at Trinity Hall, Cambridge in 1519. Many came into an experience of the 'greater work' through this little man's clear teaching from the New Testament, including Hugh Latimer, later Bishop of Worcester, whom many reckon to be the greatest preacher ever heard in the English language. Henry VIII certainly esteemed him more highly than any other preacher he ever had at court.

John Newton experienced the 'greater work' when he was converted from being a the captain of a slave-trading ship to being first a simple believer in the Lord Jesus Christ, and then later one who turned many from darkness to light by his faithful and clear preaching of Christ's gospel.

Jews have been notoriously difficult to win over to faith in Jesus of Nazareth as the Messiah and Son of God. My Jewish ancestors came to this country around 1720 from Germany. They were the first Jews to become citizens of Liverpool. My father's brother, Major F. A. Samuel, was Aide-de-Camp to General Allenby when he walked into Jerusalem on 11 December 1917 to receive the surrender of the Turkish forces. Their second cousin, later Viscount Samuel, was the first High Commissioner for the mandated Palestine from 1920-26. But my father was the first of the family to experience the 'greater work' of his spiritual eyes being opened and from 1939 till his departure for heaven in 1955 he gave the whole of his life to seeking to lead men in the forces, in the Chester area, to faith in Christ. In other words, the 'greater work' absorbed all his energies. Many will rise up in that great day that is coming and join with me in calling him 'blessed'!

It was largely due to the godly teaching which I had from my parents, and which I saw illustrated in their lives, and significantly through the crystal clear teaching and radiant living of a Dublin lawyer, Robert Matheson, who gave up his summer vacations to teach the gospel to boys and girls on the beach at Port St Mary, in the Isle of Man. that, as a teenager, I experienced this 'greater work' and my blind eyes were opened. To God be all the glory!

In some the work is seen to be very dramatic. The deeper they have been in sin, the more remarkable the change. The more pious they have been, the more godly their upbringing, the less obvious the change outwardly. But inwardly the change is as big a miracle in the well-taught as it is in those who hear the good news for the first time when they are up to their necks in sin.

Christians are not called to try to perform the great works the Saviour did in the days of his earthly three-year ministry, but we are all invited, indeed commanded (Philippians 2:12-16), to be witnesses to him who has redeemed us with his most precious blood, and to seek to do 'the greater work' of leading blind sinners into the marvellous light of our Lord Jesus Christ, as we shine in a dark world and hold forth the word of life. May God help us to fulfil this glorious role in our day and generation. Have we each told him we are available, and really willing to be used?

1. I can sing verses 2 and 3 with a good conscience.

5.
What about healing on demand?

'God must heal. He has committed himself.' 'We have only to ask in faith, and God will do it.' The many who hold this view today point to a number of scriptures in support of their position. Let me quote some.

Old Testament proof texts

In Exodus 15:26 the Lord says, 'I am the Lord, who heals you.' Some people maintain that this means the Lord will always heal all his people, of all generations, from whatever illnesses they may have. For some it rules out seeking the help of surgeons, doctors and nurses and the use of all medicines, because they must put all their faith for healing in God alone, without medical means.

In 2 Chronicles 16:12 we read of King Asa, who was suffering from diseased feet (possibly gout), 'In his illness he did not seek help from the Lord, but only from the physicians.' The moral drawn from this is that we must not consult physicians but only go to the Lord about our illnesses.

In Psalm 103:3 the psalmist encourages himself to praise 'the Lord ... who ... heals all your diseases'. Once again some people take this as an absolute statement applying to all God's people at all times.

New Testament proof texts

The key New Testament verse in the thinking of many is Hebrews 13:8: 'Jesus Christ is the same yesterday and today and for ever.' Because we read in Matthew 8:16-17 that Jesus 'drove out the [evil] spirits with a word and healed *all* the sick', and because he is still the same today, the argument goes, we have every right to expect him to do the same today, that is, to heal all the sick we bring to him. 'Anyway,' they say, 'healing is in the atonement. Christ did not only purchase the forgiveness of our sins by his atoning death; he purchased our healing, the wholeness of our bodies. Isn't that what Matthew means by quoting Isaiah 53:4: "He took up our infirmities, and carried our diseases"?'

In Acts 3 Peter healed a cripple in the name of Jesus. In Acts 9 Peter raised Dorcas from the dead. In Acts 14 Paul healed the cripple at Lystra. In Acts 20 Paul raised Eutychus from the dead. All this was done in the name of Jesus. He is the same today, so, the argument runs, we ought to be doing the same today. And because we are not doing it, people are very slow to turn to the Lord. They cannot hear our words. They are deaf to our preaching of the gospel. But they are not blind. If only we showed them signs and wonders such as we read of in the New Testament, there would be masses, not a pathetic trickle, of sinners turning to the Lord. 'Power evangelism' is the answer.

Does it work?

What happens when someone accepts this position? A healer came to Southampton. She laid hands on 300 sick people in the name of the Lord Jesus. She pronounced them all healed. The 'healed' went home with high expectations, but those expectations were quickly dashed. One young man whom I know well did as the healer said. He 'acted healed'. A bad haemorrhage in a London street led to emergency treatment in a London hospital, followed by chest surgery in a Southampton hospital. He is alive and well today in spite of the healer!

One of my closest friends was persuaded to go to a centre in Somerset where they laid hands on him. 'Do you believe Jesus

Christ is the same yesterday and today and for ever?' he was asked. Dick replied, 'Of course.' 'Do you believe he *can* heal you of your cancer?' 'Of course.' Dick was reminded by the group of the leper who said to our Lord, 'If you are willing you can make me clean.' The Lord replied, 'I will. Be clean,' and the man's leprosy vanished. This was to illustrate the Lord's expressed willingness to heal whenever asked in faith. So Dick was asked the next question: 'Do you believe he *is willing* to heal you?' In the light of the model he had been offered he said, 'Yes.' 'Will you ask him to heal you now?' Dick did so. Then they laid hands on him.

'What do I do now?' he asked. 'Act healed,' came the reply. So he drove his Jaguar up to Cader Idris and started to climb his favourite mountain. A few hundred yards up he had a haemorrhage. He dragged himself sadly back to his car and drove back to Reading with a double burden — his cancer not healed, and an overwhelming sense of guilt that he had not had enough faith. He was in that sad condition when I found him. I showed him the verses in Hebrews 11 where we read of some who by faith escaped the edge of the sword while others by faith (the same faith in the same God) were slain by the edge of the sword. It was a matter of God's sovereignty, not of their faith. Of course, God could have healed Dick of his cancer, just as he could have healed David Watson of his cancer. But he chose not to, and he was not going back on any commitments to his people when he made this choice. He was acting in love towards his servants, and doing what was best for them.

What does this promise really mean?

Let me explain what I mean by saying God was not going back on his word. When we read those wonderful words, 'Jesus Christ is the same yesterday and today and for ever,' we must not read into them more than the writer intended. Verses 5-7 give us the context. We are guaranteed his unceasing presence (as in 'Surely I am with you always, to the very end of the age') and his unfailing provision. 'God has said, "Never will I leave you; never will I forsake you"' (v. 6). As surely as our teachers (v. 7) proved this right up to the end of their lives, even if they died a martyr's death, so will we. For 'Jesus Christ is the same yesterday and today and for ever.'

But the fact that he is the same in *character and attitude* is not to be understood as meaning that he *is always repeating the same programme*. He entered the womb of the Virgin Mary. That was a one-off event. Nine months later he was born. There has been no repeat. He suffered under Pontius Pilate and was crucified. He died and was buried. On the third day he rose again from the dead. Each of these events occurred once only. The programme was not repeated. He taught his disciples, with them taking in his teaching at last in the power of the Holy Spirit (Acts 1:1-3) for forty days. Those days were not extended. He ascended once into heaven, personally and visibly, from the Mount of Olives. He is coming back again personally and visibly. That will be a once-only event too.

Peter said on the Day of Pentecost that Christ's healing miracles attested him, bore witness to him as the Messiah long expected by the Jews: 'Men of Israel, listen to this: Jesus of Nazareth was a man accredited by God to you by miracles, wonders and signs, which God did among you through him, as you yourselves know' (Acts 2:22). Those men of Israel in A. D. 30 were eyewitnesses of things we have not seen. They saw them happening. We read the inspired record of those same events, but no repeat programme is laid on for our faith to rest on.

As John says in his first epistle, 'That which was from the beginning, which *we* have heard, which *we* have seen with our eyes, which *we* have looked at and *our* hands have touched — *this we proclaim* concerning the Word of life. The life appeared; we have seen it and testify to it, and we proclaim to you the eternal life, which was with the Father and has appeared to us. We proclaim to you what we have seen and heard, so that you also may have fellowship with us' (1 John 1:1-3). John does not say, 'We are giving you a vivid description of it so that you can ask for a repeat programme of hearing with your own ears and seeing with your own eyes and touching with your own hands.' No. That salvation history programme is complete. Christ has come. Atonement for sin has been made. He died once and for all. He rose once and for all. He sits at God's right hand. He will come again to judge the living and the dead. His kingdom will never end. No plotters will organize a coup to overthrow him while he is on holiday. There are two reasons for this: he never goes 'on holiday' and no one has the power to overthrow him, not even for a few days. God is still on the throne!

But what about those proof texts?

Exodus 15:26. 'I am the Lord, who heals you' (Jehovah Rapha) is still true for the Lord's people, and he heals us of all except our terminal illness. But he usually chooses to do this through surgeons (or, as a Christian surgeon once put it, 'I make a mess of you and God heals you'), doctors and nurses, medicines, drug-therapy and diet, not forgetting remedial exercises and treatments unheard of even twenty years ago.

2 Chronicles 16:12. Christians need not feel guilty in seeking medical help as well as God's touch. The beloved physician Dr Luke was nowhere commanded to abandon his medical treatments, forget his medical training and give himself to preaching the gospel and laying hands on the sick for their recovery. He was still highly esteemed as a doctor when Paul wrote, or Paul would hardly have called him 'the beloved physician' (Colossians 4:14, AV). 'Our dear friend Luke, the doctor' is not described as the ex-doctor, or the doctor who has taken early retirement!

Matthew 8:16-17. Verse 17 is an inspired explanation of what was happening in verse 16. This exercise, at this particular time (A.D. 27-30) and in this particular place (Palestine under Roman rule) '*was to fulfil* what was spoken through the prophet Isaiah: 'He took up our infirmities, and carried our diseases.''' And whereas the quotation Matthew makes is from a chapter which unquestionably deals prophetically with the substitutionary atoning death of Christ for sinners, Matthew does not present it to the reader as an indication that physical healing is in the atonement for all men.

Matthew's words, 'This was to fulfil...,' surely point to a ministry that has already been fulfilled. In the same way, when John the Baptist sent messengers to him asking, 'Are you the one who was to come [the Messiah], or should we expect someone else?' the Lord told them, 'You must go back and tell John the signs of the Messiah [prophesied in Isaiah 35] *have been* fulfilled: the deaf hear; the blind see; dead people have been raised.' In other words, the Lord himself looked on his healing ministry as an accreditation, a visible tangible evidence that he was the Messiah and that the Messiah had come.

Matthew says nothing about healing being in the atonement, though we can say that Christ's atoning death and bodily resurrection guarantee for us a new body one day without disease or pains.

But, someone may ask, what about Peter's raising Dorcas from the dead in *Acts 9*? Our Lord had promised a select company of apostles that the works that he was doing, they would do also. Paul speaks of 'the things that mark an apostle' (2 Corinthians 12:12). If every brother or elder could have produced these signs how could anyone possibly know who was an apostle, who was accredited to give the church the mind of Christ for all generations? (1 Corinthians 14:36-38). Peter was an apostle. This was one of the marks that identified him as such.

Similarly, in *Acts 14*, Paul healed the man lame from birth at Lystra. Paul too was an apostle. The fact that he performed such a miracle does not mean that we can do the same. A visiting evangelist told the congregation of an evangelical church in Slovakia that he was going to heal a crippled woman. Many gathered to see the miracle. When the woman was not healed, the would-be healer turned on the pastor (who told me personally about the incident) saying it was his fault because he had not believed. The woman was disillusioned then but is still hoping for a miracle. Promising more than we can deliver is no help to a young church — or an older one!

In *Acts 20* Paul raised Eutychus from the dead, but, as we have already seen, this only confirms that Paul was an apostle. 'The things that mark an apostle — signs, wonders and miracles — were done' by Paul among the Corinthians (2 Corinthians 12:12). He was attested as an apostle appointed by God as surely as his Master had been attested as the Messiah sent from God.

As I mentioned in an earlier chapter, I find it fascinating that Judas, the traitor, was replaced among 'the Twelve' by Matthias, but there was no hint of finding someone to replace James when he was executed by Herod (Acts 12:2). This substantiates the New Testament evidence that the apostles were a strictly limited company.

Who was an apostle?

The Scriptures set before us five qualifications for an apostle of Christ.

1. He was chosen by the Lord himself. In Mark 3:12-16 there were only twelve, one of whom disqualified himself later. It is evident from Acts 9:15 that our Lord extended his choice to include Saul of Tarsus, who was to become Paul, the great apostle to the Gentiles: 'This man is my chosen instrument.'

2. *He was a witness of the risen Lord.* Judas' replacement was to be 'one of the men who have been with us the whole time the Lord Jesus went in and out among us ... to the time when Jesus was taken up from us' and 'must become a witness with us of his resurrection' (Acts 1:21-22). Paul asks, 'Am I not an apostle? Have I not seen Jesus our Lord?' (1 Corinthians 9:1).

3. *He was a recipient of special revelation from God.* Speaking of the Eleven, the Lord said in his high-priestly prayer, 'I have revealed you to those whom you gave me out of the world... I gave them the words you gave me and they accepted them' (John 17:6,8). Ananias told Paul, 'The God of our fathers has chosen you to know his will and to see the Righteous One and to hear words from his mouth. You will be his witness to all men of what you have seen and heard' (Acts 22:14-15). Paul wrote to the Ephesians, 'Surely you have heard about the administration of God's grace that was given to me for you, that is, the mystery made known to me by revelation...' (Ephesians 3:2-3).

4. *He was to be a foundation gift to the church.* You do not keep on laying foundations, but you do keep on building once the foundations have been laid. 'You are ... members of God's household, built on the foundation of the apostles and prophets, with Christ Jesus himself as the chief cornerstone. In him the whole building is joined together and rises to become a holy temple in the Lord. And in him you too are being built together to become a dwelling in which God lives by his Spirit' (Ephesians 2:19-22; see also Acts 2:42-47; 11:21-26).

5. Last, but not least, *an apostle of Christ was able to produce the signs of an apostle,* the things that marked him as an apostle (2 Corinthians 12:12). These miraculous signs authenticated their ministry as the divinely authorized teachers of the church, laying down all the doctrines the church needs to know in all generations until Christ, the Head of the church, returns in glory and power when the number of the elect is complete.

Truth unchanged and unchanging has been once and for all revealed through the teaching of Christ and his apostles. And this teaching, known to God from all eternity, has been disclosed and is 'now revealed and made known through the prophetic writings by the command of the eternal God, so that all nations might believe and obey him' (Romans 16:25-26). What wonderful words, inspired by our wonderful God! We come under the New Testament apostles by coming under their teaching. 'Apostolic succession' is not a matter of an unbroken succession of people who have had hands laid on them for 'authentic ordination' going right back to the apostles. It consists rather in faithfulness to the truths taught by the apostles, enshrined once for all in our New Testament.

The teaching of James

Someone may be thinking, what about the teaching of James 5:13-20 and the obligation James, the brother of our Lord, lays on elders? Is there not a Magna Carta here for the laying on of hands for the healing of the sick?

We might expect Roman Catholics to take their stand on these verses as a justification for their activities at Lourdes, in spite of the very poor record of people being helped there physically. But no! The general Roman Catholic view is that this passage is the biblical basis for 'extreme unction', when the priest is sent for in order to apply holy oil to the nostrils, eyes, ears, lips, hands and feet of a dying person — all to be applied at the last minute when a person is dying, in order to secure the up-to-date forgiveness of sins and a safe journey to heaven. Cardinal Cajetan, a Roman Catholic famous for opposing Martin Luther in 1518, said he could not find that in James 5. So two conflicting Roman Catholic views emerged.

Luther dismissed the letter of James as an 'epistle of straw' because he could not find justification by faith taught sufficiently clearly in it. But many Protestants have gone to it in recent years in the belief that it gives biblical encouragement for holding public meetings and campaigns in which healing is offered to the sick as well as salvation to the sinners. They reckon that an expectation of divine healing, whether for themselves or for someone else present, will make it easier for sinners to believe in the Redeemer. This all ties in with the 'power evangelism' advocated so widely in Britain by the now rather discredited John Wimber.

Now all who take the Bible seriously must agree that because God is God, there are no limitations to his power. He can do anything consistent with his character. He cannot lie (Hebrews 6:18). He cannot forgive sins without the shedding of blood (Hebrews 9:21). He cannot receive anyone into heaven just because they have tried to live a good life. He can only welcome the forgiven. He says so. But nothing is too hard for him. He can heal anybody of anything. And sometimes he does it today as remarkably as he did it in New Testament days. The healing of Jennifer Rees Larcombe, the daughter of the evangelist Tom Rees, is a case in point. But he has not promised to do this for every believer. Otherwise the greatly loved Joni would not still be going round in her chair. No one would dream of suggesting Jennifer had more faith in the same Saviour than Joni. Indeed, Jennifer seems to have been taken by surprise rather than reaping the reward of great faith!

But we can say about James 5, without fear of reasonable contradiction, the following points:

1. There is no warrant here for public healing campaigns.
2. The initiative lies with the sick believer, not with the elders or a visiting evangelist-cum-healer.
3. The setting is the sick person's home, not a tent or other public meeting-place.
4. It is the local elders who have to be sent for, that is, those who will know the sick person personally. They go by invitation, not as a pastoral invasion suggesting it is time the sick person did something more about it!
5. This presents a picture of mutual support and mutual encouragement. It is not just the sick person who is to confess faults and failings. 'Confess your sins to each other,' calls for mutual honesty, frank openness all round.
6. When James wrote oil was one of the main means used for the healing of sick people in the Middle East. It may have had medicinal value in the hands of the elders, as well as being symbolic of the Holy Spirit and his gracious activity.

All this is so clear in the text that it is difficult to see how believers can disagree on these points.

Now we must come to areas of obvious disagreement because of different interpretations due to Scripture not being compared with Scripture. If you look at James in total isolation, you might conclude, as many do today, that we can expect that all the sick who have hands laid on them will definitely be healed (not just 'feel a little better') in answer to 'the prayer of faith'. In that case you can announce in advance in your pre-mission publicity that God is going to heal the sick, raising a high level of excitement and expectancy. And in such an atmosphere you can be quite sure, if you are a sufferer from some sickness, disease, or disorder, that you are going to be healed if, when you go forward at the preacher's invitation, you are 'slain in the Spirit' and fall backwards into someone's waiting arms! This is visually powerful. To some it is wonderful. 'Just look at what the power of God is doing!' they say. To others it is terrifying. 'Whatever is going to happen next?' they ask.

Let me state some things as boldly as I can.

Firstly, there is absolutely no trace in the New Testament of people being 'slain in the Spirit'. It is nothing less than a fantasy to believe that this is clear unmistakable evidence of the Holy Spirit's presence or power. It is a modern 'Pentecostal' phenomenon which has no roots at all in Scripture, and seems to be quite different from people falling down spontaneously all over the place in the Methodist Revival of the eighteenth century and other revivals, since no hands were laid on those people to 'slay' them!

Secondly, there is no guarantee that anyone who is sick and is up-to-date with God and in dead earnest when they ask God for healing is sure to be healed. We must cover our earnest request with 'if it be your will, if it is really in our best interest to be healed'. 'That's a cop-out!' say some. 'You just add that to cover yourselves in case there isn't a healing.' But we must tread carefully here. Did not our Lord and Master pray in the Garden of Gethsemane, 'Father, if you are willing, take this cup from me; yet not my will, but yours be done'? Would anyone dare to say that was a cop-out? We don't have to try to be wiser than our Master.

An outstanding example of a man of great faith *not* being healed in answer to earnest prayer is seen in the life of the apostle Paul. 'Three times [on three separate occasions] I pleaded with the Lord to take it [some physical handicap] away from me. But he said to me, "My grace is sufficient for you, for my power is made perfect in weakness"' (2 Corinthians 12:7-9). Did Paul therefore reckon that he was disqualified from further service for the Lord, due to lack of faith? Not at all! Instead we read, "Therefore I will boast all the more gladly about my weaknesses, so that Christ's power may rest ["as a covering tent" is suggested by the Greek word] on me. That is why, for Christ's sake, I delight in weaknesses, in insults, in hardships, in persecutions, in difficulties. For when I am weak, then I am strong' (2 Corinthians 12:9-10). There is no suggestion here of a man constantly enjoying radiantly marvellous physical health because he is Spirit-filled and keeping in step with the Spirit, keeping in step with his risen Lord!

So we may dismiss the idea that James gives us a straightforward procedure which guarantees perfect healing to *all* who send for the elders of the church. What is he pointing to, then? Do the last two verses suggest he is referring to people who are sick because the Lord is disciplining them for sins they have knowingly committed? Is it a similar context to 1 Corinthians 11:30-32, where we read of some who were sick and some who had died prematurely so that they would not be condemned with the world on that great Day of Judgement which is surely coming?

Before we come to the final section of this chapter (which I could make much longer with case histories!) let me sound two notes of warning.

First, to those who follow the practice laid down in James 5:13-20: let me plead with you *not to raise people's expectations too high.* God may heal. He is God. He is sovereign. He can do anything. And I know of several instances when he has done so. But don't insist it *must* be healing. 'If it is your will... Otherwise, please give me grace such as you gave Paul, and grace to glory in my weakness, so long as your strength is made perfect in my weakness.' Don't let them feel, 'It's all my fault if I'm not healed.' 'Thy will be done,' is not a cop-out, but a Christian submission to God's sovereign wisdom.

Secondly, to those who have dismissed these verses as 'an early church practice, not relevant to today's church': *why not take the practice on board?* Teach it, practise it and reap rich benefits of fellowship and mutual understanding from it.

'How can you be so sure?'

In this final section I wish to set out my reasons for believing God does not intend to heal all who seek healing, no matter how earnestly they ask. My answer will be in two brief parts: first, New Testament practice that shows this and second, New Testament teaching that underlines it.

1. New Testament practice

Peter raised only Dorcas from the dead (Acts 9). He did not attempt to raise Stephen (Acts 7:54-8:4). Paul raised Eutychus from the dead (Acts 20). He did not attempt to raise James (Acts 12), nor did he attempt to raise any of the believing dead in Thessalonica. Instead he wrote words of great comfort to the bereaved.

Paul advised Timothy to take a little wine because of his stomach and his frequent illnesses (1 Timothy 5:23). Would he have written that if he believed the invariable answer to a believer's sickness was to send for the elders of the church and get a guaranteed healing?

Paul's great friend and fellow-warrior Epaphroditus nearly died, which would have given Paul sorrow upon sorrow, but God spared him. Why didn't Paul urge him to send for the elders of the church, if that was the royal road to a guaranteed healing? Was it on *the last day* that the Lord was going to raise up all who had suffered? (John 6: 40,44; cf. James 5:15).

Paul left Trophimus sick at Miletus (2 Timothy 4:20). Why did he not lay hands on him and heal him, if that was his commission? (cf. Acts 26:18-20).

We have already considered Paul's own limitations, when he was not healed in answer to prayer.

But we have further evidence that divine healing is not always God's plan for all his children.

2. New Testament teaching

That further evidence is clear teaching which might be described as 'the great not yet'.

Bodily perfection for the believer lies ahead of us. It is not to be expected yet. Romans 8:18-25; 2 Corinthians 4:14-5:5; Philippians 3:20-21; Hebrews 2:8 and 1 John 3:1-3 all teach precisely the same great truth, that the redemption of the body is not yet. Plagues and illnesses and infirmities can affect the most earnest of believers without their putting a foot wrong. 'Great calamities, grievous sicknesses just prove great sin,' said Job's comforters. The book of Job nails the fallacy.

Let us look at Romans 8:18-25: 'I consider that our present sufferings are not worth comparing with the glory that *will be* revealed in us. The creation waits in eager expectation for the sons of God to be revealed [seen in their radiant splendour]. For the creation was subjected to frustration, not by its own choice, but by the will of the one who subjected it, in hope that the creation itself will be liberated from its bondage to decay and brought into the glorious freedom [Greek, the freedom of the glory] of the children of God. We know that the whole creation has been groaning as in the pains of childbirth right up to the present time' (not just the time when Paul was writing, but to this very day as we read these lines).

So much for the fallen world we live in! What about believers? Paul goes on to tell us it is not only the fallen, rebellious world that experiences groaning and frustration: 'Not only so, but we ourselves, who have the firstfruits of the Spirit, [the Greek word for 'firstfruits', *haparché*, may refer to the birth certificate of a freeborn citizen] *groan inwardly* as we *wait* eagerly for our adoption as sons, [a Roman father would formally 'adopt' his own son in the marketplace when the boy reached sixteen, and he would take away his 'schoolboy uniform' and give him a grown-up man's toga] *the redemption of our bodies.* For in this hope we were saved. But hope that is seen is no hope at all. Who hopes for what he already has? But if we hope for what we do *not yet* have, we wait for it patiently.'

Do you see the 'not yet'? The redeemed body is something we do not yet have, a certain hope, but not a present possession. So we can expect our fair share of groaning in the old body in which we live now.

There is similar teaching, crystal clear, in 2 Corinthians 4:16 - 5:5: '*Outwardly we are wasting away,* yet inwardly we are being renewed day by day. For our light and momentary troubles are achieving for us an eternal glory that far outweighs them all. So we fix our eyes not on what is seen, but on what is unseen. For what is seen is temporary, but what is unseen is eternal. Now we know that if the earthly tent we live in [what a vivid picture of our body — this frail 'earthly tent'!] is destroyed [eliminated by death] we have a building from God [not yet!], an eternal house in heaven, not built by human hands. Meanwhile we [believers in Christ] groan, longing to be clothed with our heavenly dwelling... For while we are in this tent, we groan and are burdened [*not* are quickly healed and stop groaning!], because we do not wish to be unclothed [separated from our earthly bodies] but to be clothed with our heavenly dwelling [which will be exactly suited to our new environment and no longer subject, as this one is, to pain, infirmity and the inevitable, relentless, ageing processes], so that what is mortal may be swallowed up by life. Now it is God who has made us for this very purpose [something 'not yet' experienced by the believer who reads these words] and has given us the Spirit [a present experience for every believer in Christ] as a deposit [*arrhabon* — a deposit on a house purchase, but also used in Greece today for an engagement ring], guaranteeing what is to come,' but has *not yet* come!

While we are at home in our mortal body (v.6), we are in a body which can know pain as real as any unbeliever can feel it. But with us, it only drives us closer to Christ and makes us look forward to our new body.

Hebrews 2:8 gives us our next 'not yet': 'God left nothing [of his creation] that is not subject to him [man — vv. 6-8]. *Yet* at present we do *not* see everything subject to him. But we see Jesus ... *now* crowned with glory and honour because he suffered death.'

The holy, sinless, Son of God experienced awful, exquisite pain and suffering in his body without for one split second stepping out of his Father's will. Why should his faithful servants not suffer too? 'The disciple is not above his master.' 'A student is not above his teacher' (Luke 6:40; Matthew 10:24). 'If we endure [suffer], we will also reign with him' (2 Timothy 2:12). The suffering is now; the reigning is *not yet*!

Finally, let us consider 1 John 3:2: 'Dear friends, now we are children of God, and what we will be has *not yet* been made known. But we know that when he appears, we shall be like him, for we shall see him as he is [now].' This confirms Paul's inspired words to the Philippian believers: 'Our citizenship is in heaven. And we eagerly await a Saviour from there, the Lord Jesus Christ, who, by the power that enables him to bring everything under his control, will transform our lowly bodies so that they will be like his glorious body' (Philippians 3:20-21). A perfect, painless body awaits us, but we do not have it yet!

6.
Can we claim prosperity for all believers?

It was a very attractive idea, and it caught on like wildfire! After all, the man who wrote about it for the largest readership was pastor of the largest congregation in the world. His name was Dr Paul Yonggi-cho, and his church in Seoul, Korea, had half a million members. Someone I know well has attended his services to see for himself this remarkable phenomenon: thousands of people lining up, waiting for the thousands already in a service to come out so that they can take their places for the next service. It did not seem to make any difference which member of the staff was going to be leading or preaching.

What was it that was so attractive that Paul Yonggi-cho wrote? He taught that all believers should be well physically and prosperous financially. There are very few people who don't relish the idea of having good health, and there must be fewer still who cannot think of good ways of spending a lot more money — or at the very least, a bit more in the wallet or the bank.

Where does Dr Yonggi-cho get his ideas from? He reckons he can justify them very clearly from Scripture. But here he has to rely on one version alone, the Authorized version of the English Bible. In that translation, the second verse of the Third Epistle of John reads like this: 'Beloved, I wish above all things that thou mayest prosper and be in health, even as thy soul prospereth.' From these words he makes two major deductions: first, that we should all be enjoying good spiritual health, the soul prospering; and second, that above all things we should be prospering in things material. He understands that 'above all things' to mean that the apostle John is giving top priority to this wish or, as the margin reads, prayer.

The consequences for some who follow his teaching eagerly have been very far-reaching. I think of a wedding at which the officiating brother said, 'We command the health and prosperity of the bride.' Some present felt more than a little uneasy! I don't know how the bride felt about the word 'command'. Most Christian brides would hope that their closest friends would pray for them regularly that they would be able to do all God wanted them to do in a rebellious, fallen world. Being able to make ends meet as wise stewards of what God has entrusted to them would be very secondary, taken in their stride each day, but not taken for granted. I am persuaded that the desire to be useful in God's purposes would be far stronger in the mind of most earnest Christian brides than the desire to enjoy good health or be prosperous.

Some problems with this teaching

The exposition of 3 John 2 that guarantees prosperity gives me three problems. First, it offers more than can reasonably be expected. Second, it is a bad exegesis of the original text John wrote in Greek. Third, there are many passages of Scripture that make clear that the believer's true riches are treasures in heaven, not upon earth, and that we should not be surprised if we have to go through some pretty stormy seas on our way to the desired haven of heaven.

Let me take these problems up one by one.

First, if a preacher offers more in a service, whether a wedding service or a routine Sunday one, than is delivered, confidence in all else that he says is shaken. How can we be sure he is right about what he says is awaiting us in heaven if what he says we can expect on earth proves to be elusive, if not out of reach altogether? Forgiveness and subsequent peace, yes, these wonderful blessings are to be offered in the name of the Lord Jesus. The teaching of the Gospels blends in perfectly with that of the epistles to assure us that these twin blessings are available for any repenting sinner who comes to God in the name of his dear Son (1 John 1:7-10). Christ died for our sins (1 Corinthians 15:3). He is able to save to the uttermost extent all those who are in the habit of coming to God through him (Hebrews 7:25). But he has not promised that all believers will have a bed of roses, or an easy passage to glory. 'God has not promised skies ever blue ... roses without thorns...'

My second problem is with the exegesis of this text in 3 John. The Greek text will not stand the stress that is put upon the phrase 'above all things'. The word-by-word translation underneath the Greek words in the *Englishman's Greek New Testament* reads: 'Beloved, concerning all things I wish thee to prosper, even as prospers thy soul.' There is no support here for the idea that John's top priority in praying for the believers to whom he was writing was for their physical health and financial prosperity. Of course, he wants things to go well for them, but his first letter makes it crystal clear that our walk with the Lord is more important than anything else. The NIV translates it: 'Dear friend, I pray that you may enjoy good health and that all may go well with you, even as your soul is getting along well.' Certainly, we see here a genuine concern for the health of Gaius, the welcoming host to any believer who was passing through. But did John regard this as the most important thing in his life? No! His faithfulness to the truth and his continuing to live up to what he said he believed were far more important than his bodily health, or his financial prosperity. That is why John says just a couple of verses later, 'I have no greater joy than to hear that my children are walking in the truth' (3 John 4). That is where his priorities lie as he thinks about and prays for Gaius.

Paul Yonggi-cho teaches that health and prosperity are to be considered as the top priority for all believers. His understanding of the AV translation leads him to this conclusion. Most other evangelical commentators say, 'No, it is a wish, but not a top priority prayer.' The translation 'above all things' leads to this serious misunderstanding on the part of those who follow the Korean pastor, and others who teach the same ideas. But the *'peri panton'* of the Greek text should be rendered 'concerning all things' or ' in every respect', referring to the extent of its application rather than the degreee of priority to be accorded to it.

The witness of early church history in Acts

If the thesis of the advocates of prosperity for all believers is correct, we would expect the first champions of the Christian faith to be given a very smooth passage through life. But what do we find?

Instead, we see them facing trouble, persecution and pressure at almost every turn of the way.

Peter and John are arrested soon after the Day of Pentecost and put into jail for teaching the people the resurrection of the dead, illustrated supremely by the very recent resurrection of the Lord Jesus Christ (Acts 4:3). Not long after, in spite of performing many miraculous signs and wonders among the people, we find them arrested again by the jealous religious authorities, and put in Jerusalem's public jail (Acts 5:18). In the same chapter we read of fear seizing the whole church (Acts 5:11) because of the sudden death under God's judgement of Ananias and Sapphira, judged for pretending to be more dedicated than they were.

Having broken the ban imposed on them by the Sanhedrin, the apostles are flogged and ordered again not to speak in the name of Jesus (Acts 5:27-40). How did they react to that? They 'left the Sanhedrin, rejoicing because they had been counted worthy of suffering disgrace for the Name' (Acts 5:41). Evidently they did not sit back and ask themselves what had happened to their comfort and prosperity! The following verse tells us that 'Day after day, in the temple courts and from house to house, they never stopped teaching and proclaiming the good news that Jesus is the Christ.' This ministry was far more important to them than comfort, good health and prosperity. The gospel must be spread.

Stephen walked so closely with his risen Lord that when he faced a very hostile Sanhedrin, those looking intently at him 'saw that his face was like the face of an angel' (Acts 6:15), radiant under pressure, beautiful with heaven's peace, but that did not stop them stoning him to death. Faced with the fury of the top judicial body in the land, who were gnashing their teeth at him, he, being 'full of the Holy Spirit, looked up to heaven and saw the glory of God, and Jesus standing at the right hand of God' (Acts 7:54). He declared openly what he could see, but that did not stop them rushing at him, yelling at the top of their voices and dragging him out of the city, where they stoned him to death. There the Lord Jesus was standing to welcome him; but his last moments on earth could hardly be described as prosperous, could they?

Soon after Paul's conversion we find the Jews in Damascus conspiring to kill him. He escaped by being let down, in a fish hamper, through an opening in the wall (Acts 9:23-25). Ananias had spoken to the Lord about all the harm Saul had done to his saints in

Jerusalem, citing many reports (Acts 9:13). Ananias in turn was told to tell Saul how much he must suffer for the name of the Lord Jesus (Acts 9:16) — nothing about how comfortable life was going to be for him because he was in the throes of a wonderful conversion!

We read in Acts 12 of King Herod arresting some who belonged to the church, and of his putting James, the brother of John, to death by the sword. Next we read of Peter being arrested and put in prison, closely guarded (Acts 12:1-4). These men were the Lord's top representatives, but we see little evidence of prosperity being all that important in their experience.

The rest of Acts presents Paul as the leading figure. We find him being stoned at Lystra, and dragged out of the city for dead. The famous story of Paul and Silas in prison hardly needs telling again, although we may need to be reminded that they were stripped and severely flogged before they were thrown into prison. That did not stop them praying and singing hymns to God at midnight. Riots in Thessalonica and Ephesus further added to the discomfort of Paul and Silas (Acts 17:5-10; 19:28-41).

In his farewell address to the Ephesian elders at Miletus, Paul says, 'I have declared to both Jews and Greeks that they must turn to God in repentance and have faith in our Lord Jesus' (Acts 20:21). If ever there was a faithful minister of the gospel, Paul was that man. But was he favoured on earth with prosperity? In the very next verse, he says, 'And now, compelled by the Spirit, I am going to Jerusalem, not knowing what will happen to me there. I only know that in every city the Holy Spirit warns me that prison and hardships are facing me. However, I consider my life worth nothing to me, if only [what a wonderful "if only"!] I may finish the race and complete the task the Lord Jesus has given me — the task of testifying to the gospel of God's grace' (Acts 20:22-24). Then, having warned them of the dangers they are going to have to face from false teachers, he concludes with: 'Remember that for three years, I never stopped warning each of you night and day with tears. Now I commit you to God and to the word of his grace, which can build you up and give you an inheritance among all those who are sanctified.'

At this point he introduces an intensely interesting aside about his attitude to money, clothing, jewellery and the supply of his daily needs: 'I have not coveted anyone's silver or gold or clothing. You yourselves know that these hands of mine have supplied my own needs [working as a tent-maker, Acts 18:3] and the needs of my companions. In everything I did, I showed you that by this kind of hard work we must help the weak, remembering the words the Lord Jesus himself said: "It is more blessed to give than to receive"' (Acts 20:29-35).

Two years in prison in Caesarea and two in Rome, and a pretty scary shipwreck on the way to Rome hardly paint a picture of great comfort and prosperity. Yet, 'It is the way the Master went. Should not the servant tread it still?' 'I can face all circumstances through the Christ who is continually strengthening me' (lit. Greek) crystallizes the attitude of the great apostle to the Gentiles, a great hero of the faith, whom I look forward to meeting in the glory land.

The teaching of the epistles about what believers can expect

When we turn to the epistles we find stronger promises of suffering than of prosperity. Take, for example, Romans 8:17-26: 'Now if we are [God's] children, then we are heirs — heirs of God and co-heirs with Christ, if indeed we share in his sufferings in order that we may also share in his glory.

'I consider that our present sufferings are not worth comparing with the glory that will be revealed in us. The creation waits in eager expectation for the sons of God to be revealed. For the creation was subjected to frustration, not by its own choice, but by the will of the one who subjected it, in hope that the creation itself will be liberated from its bondage to decay and brought into the glorious freedom [literally, the freedom of the glory] of the children of God.

'We know that the whole creation has been groaning as in the pains of childbirth right up to the present time. Not only so, but we ourselves, who have the firstfruits of the Spirit, groan inwardly as we wait eagerly for our adoption as sons [namely] the redemption of our bodies. For in this hope we were saved. But hope that is seen is no hope at all. Who hopes for what he already has? But if we hope for what we do not yet have, we wait for it patiently.

'In the same way, the Spirit helps us in our weakness. We do not know what we ought to pray for, but the Spirit himself intercedes for us with groans that words cannot express ... interceding for the saints in accordance with God's will.'

Paul lists the things that Christian workers and all faithful believers can expect at the hands of the enemies of the gospel:

'trouble ... hardship ... persecution ... famine ... nakedness ... danger or [even] sword'. He concludes triumphantly with the ringing assurance that nothing, absolutely nothing 'will be able to separate us from the love of God that is in Christ Jesus our Lord' (Romans 8:36-39). But that ringing assurance brings with it no promise of an easy ride through this life. We are pilgrims. We are on a journey. At times the road will be really hard going, but he has said, 'I will never leave you nor forsake you.' His unceasing presence and his unfailing provision make the journey so worthwhile! We can cope, by his grace.

Writing to the Corinthians, Paul says, 'We do not lose heart. Though outwardly we are wasting away [not enjoying perfect health!], yet inwardly we are being renewed day by day. For our light and momentary [but none the less real] troubles are achieving for us an eternal glory that far outweighs them all.' He describes the body we are living in now as a 'tent'. It is frail, as all earthly tents are. One day it is to be exchanged for a house, but, in the meantime, 'While we are in this tent, we groan and are burdened...' (2 Corinthians 4:16-15:4). This is the genuine experience of a true servant of the Lord Jesus Christ. There is no triumphalism here. He has not arrived. There are still difficult situations to be faced. Our aim is to please the Lord in every situation, every day till he comes or calls.

Writing to Timothy, Paul states a great principle: 'Everyone who wants to live a godly life in [union with] Christ Jesus will be persecuted' (2 Timothy 3:12). This is not easy to square with the promise of prosperity for all believers, is it?

The apostle Peter has a lot to say about suffering. There is no hint that only those who step out of the will of God, or fail to lay hold of God's promises and provision for all the saints, will have to suffer as Christians: 'For it is commendable if a man bears up under the pain of unjust suffering because he is conscious of God... If you suffer for doing good and you endure it [not 'escape it'], this is commendable before God. To this you were called, because Christ suffered for you, leaving you an example, that you should follow in his steps...' (1 Peter 2:19-21). In the next chapter he says, 'It is better, if it is God's will, to suffer for doing good than for doing evil' (1 Peter 3:17).

Peter has still more to say which is totally at variance with the idea that God's purpose for his children is that they should usually be living in comfort and prosperity — if only they will believe and ask. 'Dear friends, do not be surprised at the painful trial you are suffering, as though something strange were happening to you. But rejoice that you participate in the sufferings of Christ, so that you may be overjoyed *when his glory is revealed*... If you are insulted because of the name of Christ, you are blessed, for the Spirit of glory and of God rests on you. If you suffer, it should not be as a murderer or thief or any other kind of criminal, or even as a meddler [busybody]. However, if you suffer as a Christian, do not be ashamed [or ask, "What has gone wrong with my prosperity?"] but praise God that you bear that name... Those who suffer according to God's will should commit themselves to their faithful Creator and continue to do good' (1 Peter 4:12-19).

Peter concludes his reference to the uncomfortable life Christians may well have to face in this rebellious world with a wonderful prayer which is also a promise: 'And the God of all grace, who called you to his eternal glory in Christ, after you have suffered a little while, will himself restore you and make you strong, firm and steadfast. To him be the power for ever and ever. Amen' (1 Peter 5:10-11 — a prayer in the AV, a promise in the NIV). The suffering is limited by God; the grace is unlimited from God. To him be the glory for ever!

Let me finish my quotations from Scripture with a reference to James, the brother of our Lord: 'Suppose a man comes into your meeting wearing a gold ring and fine clothes, and a poor man in shabby clothes also comes in. If you show special attention to the man wearing fine clothes and say, "Here's a good seat for you," but say to the poor man, "You stand there," or "Sit on the floor by my feet," have you not discriminated among yourselves and become judges with evil thoughts? [e.g. "The rich man must be well-pleasing to God. This poor man must have grieved him, or he would not be so poor still!"]

'Listen, my dear brothers: Has not God chosen those who are poor in the eyes of the world to be rich in faith and to inherit the kingdom he promised to those who love him?' (James 2:2-5).

The latter thought, God's sovereign choice, is in line with what Paul says to the Corinthians: '[God] chose the lowly things of this world and the despised things — and the things that are not — to nullify the things that are, so that no one may boast before him' (1 Corinthians 1:28-29; see also vv. 18-31).

Having said all this, where would the early church have been without the generosity of men like Barnabas? (See Acts 4:34-37). Not everybody, however keen they may be as Christians, can be trusted with a lot of money. Not all know how to handle it. God wants good stewardship. But in our own day, he raises up men with a flair for business, men whose wise giving, and handling of other people's giving, makes a great difference to the lives of many of his hard-working servants at home and overseas. God grant that such servants of his, wise stewards of what they have earned by diligent and wise application to their daily work, may prosper more and more. May the Lord's work go forward through their generosity. But the Scriptures do not lead us to the conclusion that all believers should above all things 'prosper financially even as their soul does'. 'My God shall supply all your need,' does not run to 'all your luxuries or desires'!

7.
What do we mean by the baptism and fulness of the Holy Spirit?

'Have you had the baptism?' is a question which has been put to many members of evangelical churches in recent days. What are we to understand by 'the baptism of the Holy Spirit'? Is it the same for believers in the Lord Jesus Christ today as it was for the first disciples on the Day of Pentecost in the year A.D. 30? Does it always come the same way? When it happened to other believers whose experience is recorded in the Acts of the Apostles did the same phenomena occur as with those who received it on the Day of Pentecost?

The baptism of the Spirit

The baptism of the Spirit is defined by different evangelical Christians today in at least three different ways. All these people believe that their view is the only correct one in accordance with the Scriptures. Each of the three groups claims very sincerely that their only desire is to be subject to Scripture, their final authority.

The first view is that the baptism is an experience subsequent to regeneration, which is evidenced by the sign or gift of speaking in tongues and by means of which a weak Christian is swiftly transformed into a powerful Christian. The second view is that it is an experience subsequent to regeneration evidenced by a great release of love for Christ and all his people, but not necessarily accompanied by tongues. The key thought in these two views is subsequence. These two views are based firmly and squarely on the experience of the very first disciples, those who were following Christ for at least part of the three years before his death and bodily resurrection.

The third view is that the baptism of the Spirit is an experience simultaneous with regeneration, whereby the new believer is invisibly incorporated into the body of Christ and receives the Holy Spirit as his or her indwelling life and source of power for living the Christian life and sharing the Christian faith. Those who understand the Scriptures in this way believe that the baptism of the Spirit happens to believers at the time of the new birth and not after it, that it coincides with reconciliation and justification and is not an experience subsequent to getting right with God.

The most crucial Scriptures for those who take this doctrinal position, believing it to fit all the Scriptures best, are 1 Corinthians 6:19-20; 1 Corinthians 12:13 and Romans 8:9.

Addressing the believers at Corinth, without singling out certain specially privileged individuals, Paul asks them, 'Do you not know that your body is a temple of the Holy Spirit, who is in you, whom you have received from God? You are not on your own; you were bought at a price. Therefore honour God with your body' (1 Corinthians 6:19-20). The body is not a prison for the soul, as most of the Greek philosophers had been teaching for centuries, nor a toy to be played with indiscriminately, as the hedonists known as Epicureans had been teaching, but a temple for the Spirit, a tent to be exchanged later for a house and in the case of married believers a piece of jointly owned property, belonging first and foremost to God (2 Corinthians 5:1-5; 1 Corinthians 7:2-9).

Further on in the same epistle Paul writes, 'For we were all baptized by one Spirit [Greek, "in one Spirit"] into one body — whether Jews or Greeks, slave or free — and we were all given the one Spirit to drink' (1 Corinthians 12:13).

In his epistle to the Romans he states plainly that 'If anyone does not have the Spirit of Christ, he does not belong to Christ,' or, to quote the AV, 'he is none of his' (Romans 8:9).

We must face the fact that many believers are under pressure from other believers. They are confused. They don't know what to believe about these things. And it is not only Protestants who are confused. Some who would call themselves Catholic Pentecostals are teaching that the baptism in the Spirit happened to them at their infant baptism, when they believe they were regenerated, and that the subsequent experience they have had in the Catholic Pentecostal movement is nothing more than the realization in their experience of what was made truly theirs by their baptismal regeneration in infancy.

It is inevitable that anyone who has been mixing with Christians for more than a few months should come to this chapter with some preconceived ideas. I hope that you who are reading this book will be prepared to take a fresh look at the Word of God, trying to put aside your prejudices and preconceived ideas. Whatever view you may embrace as your 'position', I trust you will hold it in love, and not in anger, or in scorn of sincere people who do not see eye to eye with you. We must respect our brethren who take a different view from our own, bearing in mind that most, if not all, of these are seeking to be subject only to Scripture as they understand it.

Under the influence of R. A. Torrey's writings and some of the Keswick reports and that of friends whose discipleship I admired in my student days, the phrase 'the baptism of the Spirit' used to warm my heart. I used to believe it described an extra experience which every Christian, not just preachers, needed after regeneration. But my understanding of this phrase has changed radically over the years through my continued study of Scripture as a whole.

How does the Bible use this expression?

To start with, the noun phrase, 'the baptism of the Spirit' does not occur once in the Scriptures, and while the passive verb translated from the Greek by 'baptized in the Spirit' does occur, it only occurs three times, and never as a command to seek this experience.

Firstly, it was promised as a future experience through the lips of John the Baptist (Matthew 3:11; Mark 1:8; Luke 3:16; John 1:33).

Secondly, it was promised by the risen Lord himself during the forty days of intensive teaching which he gave to the apostles before his ascension. He made clear to them that the promise was to be fulfilled very shortly (Acts 1:5). At the moment of his reiterating this promise he was referring to an imminent experience, something to be expected very soon; no other believers have ever been instructed by him to go to the city of Jerusalem and wait for the Spirit to come in power — though doubtless some subsequently have thought they were! However, the event has not fulfilled their hopes as it did for the disciples on that wonderful Day of Pentecost.

Thirdly, the passive verb, being 'baptized in the Spirit', is used with reference to all believers, at least all believers in Corinth, as a past experience, not something that would solve all their problems or make them 'topped-up Christians', but that had brought them into the one body of Christ (1 Corinthians 12:13, which has already been quoted). We should also compare Galatians 3:26-29, which says, 'You are all sons of God through faith in Christ Jesus, for all of you who were baptized into Christ have been clothed with Christ. There is neither Jew nor Greek, slave nor free, male nor female, for you are all one in Christ Jesus. If you belong to Christ, then you are Abraham's seed and heirs according to the promise.'

If we look carefully at the first two chapters of Acts, I doubt if any of us would have any hesitation in agreeing that when the Lord Jesus spoke of 'in a few days' he was referring to the Day of Pentecost. Indeed, Peter states plainly that what took place that momentous day was the fulfilment of Joel's prophecy: 'This is what was spoken by the prophet Joel: " ... I will pour out my Spirit on all people"' (Acts 2:16-17 cf. v. 33).

The main subject I studied for my degree at Liverpool University was Hellenistic Greek, the language in which the New Testament was originally written. So the consistent use of the preposition 'in' with reference to the Spirit in the Greek text is highly significant to me. This is to be seen in each of the references to being baptized in the Spirit, few though they are. John the Baptist says, 'He [the Messiah] will baptize you *in* the Holy Spirit.' The AV and NIV say '*with*' the Holy Spirit. In passing let us note that it is Christ, and not the Spirit, who is identified as the one who baptizes. Similarly in 1 Corinthians 12:13 where the AV and NIV say, '*by* one Spirit' the same Greek word for 'in' is used: '*In* one Spirit you were all baptized into one body...'

As we compare Scripture with Scripture we may conclude three things: Christ himself is the one who baptizes in the Holy Spirit; all believers, not just a special few, have been baptized in the one Spirit; and, thirdly, through this baptism we are brought into the body of Christ alongside all other believers, no matter what our race or social status, spiritual attainment or spiritual condition or spiritual gifts.

This was true even of all the believers in Corinth, with all their problems, moral, spiritual, social and otherwise.

Every Christian possesses the Spirit

Nowhere in Scripture, as I hinted earlier, do we find a command to 'be baptized in the Spirit', but there is a very plain statement to the effect that every Christian already possesses the Holy Spirit: 'If anyone does not have the Spirit of Christ, he does not belong to Christ' (Romans 8:9)

If, then, we meet someone who is wondering whether or not he or she has received the Holy Spirit as a person, let us point this person to this great touchstone of biblical teaching. As we have seen in an earlier chapter, the greatest miracle in the world today is re-generation. Its consequences last for ever. Regeneration is nothing less than that mighty miracle of God by which a person is not only given something of the very life of Christ, new life through the Holy Spirit, but by which that same Holy Spirit comes to take up residence in that person's spirit. By the same Holy Spirit and in that same moment he or she is incorporated into the mystical body of Christ, the church. These people were in Adam, in solidarity with the rebellious and lost human race. They are now in Christ, in solidarity with the whole body of redeemed people from all generations. At one time when I was asked, 'Have you had the baptism of the Holy Spirit?' I used to say, 'It depends entirely on what you mean,' but now I reply without any hesitation, 'Yes, thank God.'

When we say that every Christian has been baptized in the Spirit, we are not to be thought of as saying that 'There is nothing more of the Holy Spirit's working to be experienced by the Christian beyond regeneration.' But we must take great care not to minimize that mighty miracle whereby a self-centred rebel is brought out of spiritual darkness into the glorious light and life of God's family circle, with all the wonderful prospects that lie ahead for every believer in our Lord Jesus.

No matter what view we take of the phrase 'the baptism of the Spirit', no doubt we are all agreed that we continually need the Holy Spirit's powerful working in our lives to make us more like Christ. It is a sad reflection on evangelical church life today that far too many of us show far too little of the fruit of the Spirit in our everyday lives and in situations that arise in our churches.

What do we make of claims to special experiences?

I am not calling into question the personal experiences of great Christians who were mightily used by God in bygone days. Some well-known missionaries with very little opportunity for hearing others minister from God's Word have had on occasion remarkable touches of God's Holy Spirit on their lives. They may have called this 'a baptism of the Holy Spirit' or 'a fresh baptism of the Holy Spirit'. I am not for a moment questioning the reality of these experiences or their source. What I am asking is whether they have given their experience the correct name. Have they described it in the most biblical way? Or are they confusing their hearers or readers by the terminology they are using? Might it not, for instance, be better described as an anointing or 'a fresh anointing of the Holy Spirit'? The New Testament speaks of the Saviour being anointed for his ministry in Palestine (Luke 4:18; Acts 10:38).

Of course, there are others who claim to have had experiences as to which we may seriously question whether they have anything at all to do with the Holy Spirit of God. 'By their fruits you shall know them,' said the Saviour.

There are those who tell us that unless we have had what they call a 'post-conversion baptism of the Spirit' we cannot know anything of the joy and love and power of a genuine Christian life. From my personal observation I have no hesitation in saying that many who claim to have had this supposedly all-transforming experience have found that without frequent restirring of the emotions they all too easily sink into depths of depression and doubt. One girl, who had spoken in tongues but now has no time for Christian things, said not long ago, 'Get away from the group and it doesn't work.'

The fulness of the Spirit

While there is no command in the New Testament, 'Be baptized in the Spirit', there is a very clear command in Ephesians 5:18: 'Be filled with the Spirit.' This is the will of God for all his children. Every Christian possesses the Spirit, but not every Christian is possessed by the Spirit, even though all believers belong to the Father, the Son and the Holy Spirit (Romans 8:9; Galatians 5:13-16).

Every Christian is indwelt by the Spirit, and has been sealed by the Spirit, marked off as belonging to Christ (Ephesians 1:13-14; 2 Corinthians 1:22) but not all show clear evidence of this every day and in every situation. The first disciples were filled with the Holy Spirit. Their message was full of Christ. In the outline of Peter's sermon recorded in Acts 2, we have no less than twenty-four references to Christ; and no less than 3,000 Jews from all over the Roman world turned to Christ and were baptized as believers that day. We read that the same disciples were again filled not long after (Acts 2:4-39; 4:31-33). Being filled with the Holy Spirit is not just a bright idea put forward by some enthusiastic preachers. It is not just an optional extra for those who are going to be full-time Christian workers. It is a 'must' for every Christian. If we are to be obedient children we must be filled with the Spirit.

What exactly is meant by the phrase, 'Be filled with the Spirit'? The present imperative tense in the Greek indicates that we are called, indeed commanded, to 'go on being filled in the Spirit'. There is no such thing as a once-for-all fulness. The phrase 'in the Spirit' refers to the energy by which the Christian is to live, move and have his being, as well as the atmosphere he is to breathe moment by moment. The Greek preposition 'in' used here is the strongest way of expressing agency, the strongest way of saying 'by'. The Holy Spirit is not just coming to fill us with himself; he is coming to fill us with Christ. The command of Ephesians 5:18 is totally in line with the prayer of Ephesians 3:14-21. This is that we may be strengthened with might by his Spirit in our inner man in order that Christ may really and truly be at home in our hearts by faith. We all know it is one thing to be in somebody's house, and quite another thing to be at home there. The verb used in Ephesians 3:17 does not just speak of Christ being present, in residence, but of his being really at home *(katoikeo)*. The Holy Spirit brings the Father too (John 14:23). We do not have to receive the Father separately. Think of it — we are to be a resting-place for the Father, Son and Holy Spirit on earth, and a launching-pad for them to move out into the lives of others! How important then for each of us to be available for God every day, made clean and usable afresh!

What are the effects of being filled with the Holy Spirit?

What consequences can we expect according to the Scriptures, irrespective of experiences some other people may claim? We shall begin with two negatives. Firstly, there is no encouragement to expect overwhelming emotion, or an ecstasy that lifts us right out of this world, nor even a sense of power, though we may well find we can speak more freely of Christ than ever before. That surely is in line with the promise in Acts 1:8. Secondly, speaking in an unknown tongue is not an incontrovertible proof that I have been filled with the Holy Spirit. Many non-Christians have been able to produce this phenomenon. With some it is satanic in origin, with others merely psychological.

However, when we look at the context of Ephesians 5 we have little difficulty in finding certain characteristics which will mark the life of the Spirit-filled Christian.

1. The mutual encouragement of fellow-believers (v. 19). We have something to say to them: an up-to-date testimony to the Lord's goodness to us, or perhaps some part of Scripture that he has made to come alive to us.

2. An inward joyfulness that is independent of circumstances (v. 19). 'Happiness happens, but joy abides in the heart that is stayed upon Jesus.' A joyful Christian is not feverishly seeking an experience, or constantly seeking blessing, but he or she will be on the look-out for every opportunity to seek the Lord. He does not send us to the Spirit for himself. Instead he calls us to himself for the Spirit to flow forth from us like rivers of living water (John 7:37-39).

3. Continual thankfulness to our heavenly Father (v. 20), whatever the circumstances in which we find ourselves. We all know how uplifting it is to be in the presence of thankful people. They do us so much good. Their very laughter is a benediction! And we all know how miserable the grumblers can make us. Most of us long to take evasive action when we see a chronic grumbler bearing down upon us! Even if we lack the courage to run away, we must own up to the desire! You cannot be Spirit-filled if you are for ever grumbling! But if you are Spirit-filled you will always be able to find something to thank God for.

4. 'Submitting to one another' (v. 21). This means a genuine humility which considers other people and does not encourage us to stand on our own rights. This evidence of the Spirit's fulness will be seen in a mutual submissiveness which leads to good relationships in the home, in the church and at work. In marriage the evidence of the Spirit's fulness is seen in the husband who is loving and affectionate, tender and sensitive, who does not just feel love deep down, but expresses it in words and looks. It is seen in the wife who does not dominate her husband, but takes great care of him (vv. 22-33). It is seen in children, even those who are grown-up, in the respectful attitude they show towards their parents.

The Spirit-filled person is not concerned to talk about himself or his experience so much as about Christ and his many heart-warming people. He will continually be studying the Word of God to learn more of God's will and his ways. It is fascinating to note that in Colossians 3 and 4 precisely the same consequences flow from the Word dwelling in us richly as are set before us in Ephesians 5 and 6 as evidences of being filled with the Spirit. Faithfulness to the Word without dependence on the Spirit can produce barren fundamentalists. Looking for the Spirit without diligent searching of the Scriptures daily can produce mystics. But if we come to the Word in search of our risen Lord and his healthy truth (sound doctrine) and rely on his Spirit to make the Word live to us, and make us live in the light of that Word, then we will be the sort of Christians God is looking for today.

What are we looking for in the Christian life? Some remarkable experience of deliverance that will sparkle in the annals of church history? Something that could only be attributed to angelic or divine agency? A quick and final (before death!) rescue out of all our troubles? A miraculous healing? An amazing transformation overnight by which we become Christians with mighty power and an ever-increasing reputation?

I have such vivid memories of the first man who said to me, 'I must have power.' He went here, there and everywhere in pursuit of this power. English hands, Welsh hands, American hands were all laid on him. At last he was able to assure me that he had received the power. I asked him what his wife thought about his new experience. He blushed. The relationship he had with her was not one tiny bit better. Nor was he cutting ice with the people he had sought to influence for Christ before.

Some common fallacies

There is much fantasy around in evangelical circles these days that simply does not tally with biblical realism. Let me mention some of the fallacies found among this fantasy:

1. The Spirit-filled Christian will *never* suffer from depression. He or she will always be 'on top', in sparkling form.

2. The Spirit-filled Christian will *often* have remarkable deliverances from danger. Each one would be able to write a book about his or her experiences, and you may be sure the book would make fascinating reading.

3. The Spirit-filled Christian can *expect* to see visions of God and of heaven and will *often* be in a state of ecstasy, or at least on the way to such an out-of-this world condition.

4. The Spirit-filled Christian is *very rarely* ill or suffering from the limitations of any physical or mental infirmity. And physical problems which do arise can quickly be dealt with by means of supernatural healing, and that without too much delay. Usefulness must not be hindered! (We have already discussed this point in the chapter on healing.)

5. The Spirit-filled Christian, being utterly yielded to Christ, is *always* a powerful personality, radiating health, exuding vitality and bubbling over with energy. Tiredness is not a word in his vocabulary.

6. The Spirit-filled Christian *never* has a trace of fear or any visible signs of weakness, whatever the circumstances, personal or social, national or international.

The biblical reality

When we turn from these glowing ideas to the New Testament, what a different picture we find! Biblical realism lends no support to these fantasies. If ever there was a man full of the Holy Spirit, that man was the great apostle Paul. But listen to his own words: 'If I must boast, I will boast about the things that show my weakness' (2 Corinthians 11:30). He goes on to speak of an experience he had as long ago as fourteen years past when he heard in paradise things man is not permitted to tell. But he says he must refrain from speaking boastfully, 'so that no one will think more of me than is warranted by what I do or say'. He then goes on to speak about his thorn in the flesh, probably an eye problem, which did not disappear even after three times of pleading. Three times the same answer was given to him from heaven: '"My grace is sufficient for you, for my power is made perfect in weakness." Therefore I will boast all the more gladly about my weaknesses, so that Christ's power may rest upon me. That is why, for Christ's sake, I delight in weaknesses, in insults, in hardships, in persecutions, in difficulties. For when I am weak, then I am strong' (2 Corinthians 12:1-10).

Someone may ask, 'What was the matter with Paul?' The answer is, 'Nothing at all.' This is New Testament Christianity. This is Spirit-filled living. This is the real image of a Spirit-filled man. Holy Spirit power is God's power using our human weakness as a platform on which it can clearly be seen to be God's power; God's power using our frail lives as lamp-holders for his light to shine into the hearts of men and women around us. God's power as a tent surrounding us, supporting the framework of the weakness of our ordinary human nature. The weakness of our humanity remains; the power of God transcends it. Have we put our weakness at the Lord's disposal? Are we each available for him to make his strength perfect in our weakness? Are we displaying more and more of the fruit of the Spirit? That is the real Spirit-filled life.

8.
Should all speak in tongues?

Until the 1960s in the English-speaking world speaking in tongues
was only to be found in circles known as Pentecostal. However,
there had been spates of the exercise of this phenomenon at different
times in church history.

The Montanists in the latter half of the second century were fully
persuaded that all Christians would be able to speak in tongues. As
we saw in chapter 1, their leader, Montanus, had not been a Christian
very long before he declared that he was the prophet God had
appointed for all Christians of his generation to listen to. In this way
they would hear God's Word for his people then alive. He announced that the New Jerusalem was about to appear, and the God-
given signal for the imminence of this impending event was to be a
new outpouring of the Holy Spirit. He claimed that his followers
belonged to a superior class of spiritual Christians, and the evidence
of this was that they were able to speak in tongues and prophesy.
They had to pull out of the world in preparation for the coming of
the Lord, observed special fast days and were briefed to expect
persecution, which would act as a refining fire to prepare the Lord's
people to become a bride-people ready for the coming of her
heavenly Bridegroom. Opposition did indeed come from the official church leaders, such as Pope Eleutherus, and in A.D. 230 they
were virtually excommunicated when the Synod of Iconium de-
cided not to recognize the validity of Montanist baptism.

John Calvin was troubled in his day by the people he described
as 'Enthusiasts', who also reckoned they had a hot-line from

heaven. They claimed that they were hearing the voice of the Holy Spirit speaking to them directly, so that they no longer needed the dependence on the Scriptures which marked those who were following the biblical expositions of John Calvin. Ours is not the first generation by any means to be faced with such claims. Calvin went to great pains to show that the voice of the Holy Spirit was to be heard in his day speaking through the Holy Scriptures.

Is all modern tongues-speaking really of the devil, as some claim, or is it, as others teach, a 'must' for all Christians who want to go all the way with the Lord? Or is it in most instances a means of psychological release obtained by a technique anyone can learn? The practice of speaking in tongues is by no means restricted to Christians. In spite of the often angelic look on the faces of those carried away by the utterance of strange sounds that bear no relationship to any known language when analysed in a university linguistic laboratory, more than one godly minister maintains that this practice is inspired by the devil. Medicus Simplex has maintained in a Christian Medical Fellowship publication that the string of meaningless syllables heard in modern tongues-speaking is nothing more nor less than gibberish. Professor William Samarin was able to teach eight of the students in his linguistic department in the University of Toronto how to acquire the technique without any religious connections at all. The fact that a person speaks in tongues therefore can hardly be pressed as evidence that he or she has been filled with the Spirit![1]

As in all matters of belief and behaviour, we must submit to the Scriptures as our final authority. We must examine carefully every passage that deals with any given subject, consider the context, and compare Scripture with Scripture prayerfully as well as carefully. We must also seek to evaluate the importance of any subject in the light of the way the Bible presents it.

New Testament references to speaking in tongues

There are only three instances of speaking in tongues recorded in Acts. These are found in chapters 2, 10 and 19. There can be one very clear conclusion drawn from the record in Acts 2: it was a clear sign that God was willing to accept worship in any language, not just in Hebrew or Aramaic. And the speaking was 'as the Spirit gave them utterance' (v. 4, AV). To be strictly technical it was xenolalia, not glossalalia. It was speaking in known languages that were foreign to the speakers but immediately recognizable by some hearers. No interpretation was needed. This was a major turning-point in church history. Indeed, it was the birth of the New Testament church. There is no suggestion that those who 'spoke in tongues' on these occasions formed the habit of speaking in languages unknown to them for the rest of their lives. This supernatural, uncontrived experience was a sign that the gospel blessings were as much for the Gentile world as for the Jews. I believe the Lord's promise recorded in Mark 16:17, 'They will speak in new tongues,' that is, 'in fresh languages', was fulfilled on the Day of Pentecost, the day when a church was born which was to be made up of men and women, boys and girls, from all nations.

The only other references in the New Testament to speaking in tongues are found in the three chapters in Paul's first letter to the Corinthian church, a church simply bristling with problems, hardly to be held before twentieth-century readers as a model for all Christians to follow. There is complete silence on the subject in the other teaching epistles — not even so much as a slight hint as to how Timothy and Titus are to handle the subject in the Pastoral Epistles addressed to them and containing important guidelines as to how to help the young churches in Ephesus and Crete.

We come to a most vital question: were the 'tongues' Paul was writing about to the Corinthians exactly the same sort as those we read of in the Acts? Were they intelligible languages, meaningful to some who heard? Or were they ecstatic utterances needing interpretation from a man with another gift, 'the interpretation of tongues'?

It is my conviction that they were not the same. There seems to me to be a clear distinction between them as I study these passages. I have come to this conclusion in spite of the reasoning of a Christian doctor for whom I have the most profound respect, having learned much from him both of sound theology and accurate church history in the past. He, and many other evangelicals beside him, believes the tongues in Acts and 1 Corinthians are identical, regarding the tongues in each case as the supernatural ability to speak in identifiable known languages which the speakers have not learned the hard way. Here are my reasons for believing what I do.

Firstly, in Acts 2 *the languages used by the apostles were meaningful and comunicated effectively to those who heard them*

(v. 6). They spoke in every man's dialect. The English word 'dialect' comes directly from the Greek word used in verse 6, and indicates the usage and pronunciation of a language peculiar to a particular locality or group of people. We still speak of 'local dialects'. This means speaking without a foreign accent, without misusing idioms and without using stilted, formal language that would, or could be, rather mystifying to ordinary hearers. The apostles used everyday colloquial language to convey God's eternal and glorious truths. The great crowds of foreigners gathered at Jerusalem for the Festival of Pentecost gave an outstanding opportunity to reach great multitudes who would take home with them the exciting good news of what God had done so recently in his Son's terrible death and glorious resurrection. By contrast, in 1 Corinthians 14:2 the language used is not known by anybody listening: 'No one understands him, he utters mysteries.' Unless there is someone present with the gift of interpretation, the mysteries remain unravelled, for the speaker does not know what he has been saying.

Secondly, in Acts 2 *we are told what they said, how they were enabled to say it and what the purpose was*. The same Greek word, *'glossa'*, was used to refer to the 'little member' of our body with which we can do so much harm or so much good. It was also used to indicate a meaningful language, or in the sense of 'local peculiarities of speech' or sub-dialects. Luke tells us that the purpose of the utterances on the Day of Pentecost was to glorify God in telling aloud what wonderful things he had done (v. 11). As we have already suggested, the effect would be to let everybody know that all the blessings of the gospel were for everybody, wherever they lived, whatever language might be their mother tongue. The effect was obviously also to prepare the way for Peter to reach people most effectively with the message he had to proclaim on behalf of all the apostles, and above all on behalf of his risen Lord. Evangelistic outreach was prominent, and some 3,000 conversions are recorded — perhaps as many as one in three, or as few as one in thirty, of the multitudes thronging the temple area.

The words used by the 120 (Acts 1:15; 2:1) in languages or dialects not learned by them previously (Acts 2:4-11) may possibly have been pre-eminently words of praise addressed to God, rather than primarily words of proclamation and persuasion addressed to men. We cannot be sure, as all we have is, literally, 'We do hear them speak, every man in his own dialect, the wonderful works of God,' which we may be sure included reference to the atoning death and bodily resurrection of the Saviour. But there is no uncertainty about what Peter said. We have a brilliant outline in verses 13-40. His words were instrumental in the conviction and conversion of those thousands. A careful examination of the context suggests to me that the object of the utterance of Acts 2:4 was not to create fresh warmth and deepen the devotion of a comparatively small group of believers, but to build a bridge to the vast numbers outside in obedience to their risen Lord's commission (Luke 24:47-49) and in fulfilment of his gracious promise (Acts 1:8). By contrast, in 1 Corinthians 14:2 the stated purpose is devotional, with no conversions recorded, or indeed, to be expected.

Thirdly, in Acts 2 *the subject was known* (v. 11) even if we only have the very briefest summary in the words, 'the wonders of God', or 'the wonderful works of God'. Luke also uses the same Greek word for Mary's description of her miraculous conception, translated 'great things' in Luke 1:49. What God had done through the Lord Jesus is outlined in Acts 2, where we find twenty-four references to Christ, and Acts 10:36-43, where Peter, speaking this time in Caesarea in the house of Cornelius, once again makes twenty-four references to Christ. Strange as it may seem, the apostle Paul makes a similar number of references to Christ when preaching in Pisidian Antioch. The 'wonderful works of God' are clearly centred in the Lord Jesus Christ, and if we take these sermon outlines as a fair sample of apostolic preaching we may conclude that the preaching of Spirit-filled preachers will pre-eminently focus on Christ and not on the Spirit. The Father is delighted when the Son is given the place of honour; so is the Holy Spirit. By contrast, in 1 Corinthians 14 the subject is not known unless someone with the gift of interpretation is present, or the speaker himself is given the supernatural ability to translate his unknown utterance into his own language. This is something that I find Greek evangelicals today look on as a sin against love! They reckon the time could be used so much better for the majority of the folk attending the meetings.

Fourthly, *the experience* of Acts 2 *led to all believers being edified* and the Scriptures being made to live to all (vv.16-21), but in 1 Corinthians 14:4 only the speaker is edified while this gift is being exercised.

Finally, in Acts 2 it would seem that *at least fifteen languages were involved* (vv. 8-11,14,37) as the Spirit enabled all present to speak (v. 4). All the language groups represented in Jerusalem at the time were to be reached. No national or ethnic group was to be excluded from the benefits of the gospel. By contrast, in 1 Corinthians 14:27-28,34 definite limits were placed on the use of 'tongues': no more than two, or at most three, in any public gathering or at any session; they were not to be used at all in church gatherings without an interpreter being present; and, as with prophesying, no woman was to use them at all in public gatherings of the church. Christ chose men to lead in his churches.

We do not meet so many in the nineties who insist that speaking in tongues is the one unmistakable sign that we have been filled with the Spirit. There is no evidence that those converted to Christ on the Day of Pentecost spoke in tongues, either before or after water baptism as believers. The tongues were a sign, not for the apostles that they had been blessed, but for their unbelieving hearers, that the blessing was for them, that is, the twin blessing of the forgiveness of sins and the gift of the Holy Spirit, now to be proclaimed to the whole wide world (Acts 2:38-47).

Two important questions about tongues

Firstly, how can anyone be certain that their speaking in tongues has anything to do with a life of godliness or their relationship with God, unless they or someone else knows for sure what is being said? Feelings of peace about it are not enough. Buddhists speak in tongues and claim feelings of peace. So do some Hindus. A young schoolteacher who had just started to speak in tongues as a Christian told us his Buddhist uncle had just started to do the same. It would have been fascinating if samples of both had been tape-recorded and compared in a linguistic laboratory. As I mentioned earlier, samples of tongues-speaking sent to university linguistic researchers have never so far been identifiable with any known language, nor even had a language structure. They were just pleasant sounds. But tonal likenesses have frequently been noted where there is a strong personality leading a group of 'tongues-speaking' Christians, the tones of the whole group seeming to follow those of the leader.

Secondly, how important is it? The fantasy held by many, who are called 'evangelical' by the media and others, is that speaking in tongues is a sign of being baptized in the Spirit, and that this is a 'must' for all Christians who want to 'go on with the Lord'. When Paul states so clearly that tongues are not a sign for believers (1 Corinthians 14:22, and therefore not a sign of 'the baptism'), how is it that we do not all take his word as clear and authorative and sufficient? And how is it that all Christians do not embrace Paul's evaluation of tongues-speaking when he says, 'I would rather speak five intelligible words to instruct others than ten thousand in an unknown tongue' ? (1 Corinthians 14:19).

Nowhere in the New Testament is tongues-speaking encouraged either as a gift to be displayed constantly, a spiritual ability to be exercised constantly, or a proof that the Spirit is resident in power. Whereas Paul does say, 'Be eager,' or 'Earnestly desire to prophesy' he nowhere says, 'Earnestly desire to speak in tongues' (see 1 Corinthians 14:39). The ability to 'speak in tongues', as described in 1 Corinthians 14, comes under many restrictions. Indeed, we may say it is surrounded with a hedge of biblical negatives. We must not lose sight of the fact that everything in this chapter is as inspired as the rest of the Holy Scriptures, and in verse 37 Paul says categorically that anyone who is inspired by God's Holy Spirit will recognize that the things he writes here are not just his private opinions but the commandments of God.

Biblical negatives surrounding tongues-speaking

We may find no less than fifteen negatives about the use of this gift in 1 Corinthians 14.

1. It was not on a par with prophesying, because it did not edify other Christians (vv. 2-3).

2. It was not a gift to be desired like prophesying (v. 5).

3. Using this gift was not meaningful, like a trumpet-call to battle whose note no one could mistake (v. 8).

4. It was not fruitful for the Christian's understanding, that is, for his conscious mental enjoyment and appreciation of the things of God (v. 14).

5. It was not helpful for those who did not know what was being said to hear it being used. How could they possibly say an intelligent 'Amen' to words they had not understood, even if those words were of the purest thanksgiving? (vv. 16-23).

6. The exercise of this ability in public was not the best use of the church's time (v. 19). Paul's inspired words here are very strong, and that is why the Greek evangelicals feel so strongly about this.

7. It was not a mark of the user's spiritual maturity (v. 20).

8. It was not to be given much scope in meetings of the church in case unbelievers listening should come to the conclusion that all Christians are mentally unbalanced and say, 'You are mad!' (v. 23).

9. It did not bring conviction of sin to non-Christians (v. 25).

10. It was not to be used in the church without an interpreter (v. 28).

11. The use of the gift was not to be allowed to get out of control. God is not the author of disorder (Greek 'unquietness', v. 33).

12. As with the gift of prophesying, this gift was not to be exercised by women in church gatherings (v. 34). Can we explain this ban by a shrug of the shoulders and a sad sigh for the culture of Paul's day and part of the world if we take the last sentences of this chapter seriously?

13. The passage from 12:31 - 13:13 underlines once again that the use of such tongues was not a mark of spiritual maturity or Holy Spirit reality.

14. It is not the prime or the only incontrovertible evidence that someone has had what some call the 'baptism of the Spirit' (vv. 14-22).

15. However, the use of the gift is not to be forbidden or ruled out as being always wrong in any situation, or always psychological, always dangerous or all of the devil (v. 39).

The gift is clearly played down, but the use of it is not banned altogether. It may have a place in the life of some Christians — but not all! (1 Corinthians 12:30).

A word of warning

It is important to note the emphasis that Paul places on the doctrinal content of what is said when people claim to be speaking under the direct inspiration of the Holy Spirit (1 Corinthians 12:1-3).

Tongues-speaking was practised under demonic influence in pagan temples in Corinth and elsewhere in Greece before any Christians ever started speaking in tongues (see 1 Corinthians 12:1-3). We may have heard stories of people speaking terrible blasphemies in a language that someone present happens to know. On the other hand, we may have heard of someone speaking to an unconverted person in his or her native tongue, which the speaker has never learned the hard way. I don't think we should put too much weight on either sort of such very exceptional reports, which often come to us at third or fourth hand. There is not a shadow of doubt that the Wycliffe Bible Translators would be absolutely delighted if they could be given language direct in a supernatural way instead of having a ten-year slog each time.

One alarming feature about certain advocates of 'speaking in tongues' has been the technique recommended to those who feel it important to speak in tongues, but have had difficulty in doing so. This proceeds as follows:

1. 'Let your tongue go in baby-sounds.'
2. 'Join hands in a circle with others seeking the blessing.'
3. 'Massage your tonsils' (this was advice from a well-known evangelical).
4. Pressure is then applied: 'If you haven't spoken in tongues you will be out of the battle in five years' time.' To back up their warning, leaders have been known to go round laying hands on each in the circle, and if necessary to lay hands more than once on the same people before they produce sounds beyond their control.

What place should we give to tongues today?

Surely we should give it the place that Scripture gives to it.

1. There is no command to seek this gift or to exercise it regularly. We do, however, have a clear command to observe the Lord's Supper.
2. It comes at the end of the only scriptural list in which it appears, which suggests that it is not to be put at the top of

gifts to be sought. He who inspires Scripture does not make mistakes. He is the Spirit of truth.

3. The gift was for certain individuals, not for every believer. We do not have the right to reduce the nine gifts of 1 Corinthians 12 to one, or to take the eighth in the list and make it the most important.

4. Unlike faith, hope and love, it is mentioned in only one epistle, and that the letter addressed to the only church described as carnal. The church in Corinth was more problem-ridden than any other New Testament church, and the prominent place given to tongues was one of its biggest problems.

5. It is persistently and consistently contrasted unfavourably with prophecy or prophesying (1 Corinthians 14).

6. It is to be tested (compare 1 John 4:1-6 with 1 Corinthians 12:3): 'Test the spirits.' It may be of God (giving praise), or of Satan (uttering terrible things), or of the human psyche (uttering noises which are meaningless but give psychological relief. Some would claim the 'meaningless noises' are angel's tongues).

7. 'Forbid not to speak in tongues.' Where should we speak in tongues? Edification is the great test of the best use of the church's time. Tongues do not edify others, no matter how exciting or musical they may sound. So if they must be used their best use is in private for devotional purposes. A missionary friend told me, 'I prayed in tongues regularly in India, and then realized I had become truly lazy in prayer. I hadn't a clue what I was saying, so I gave it up and came back to the harder way of prayer, with great peace of mind.'

Tongues tend to draw attention to the medium rather than to the Mediator, Christ. They emphasize the manner of speaking rather than the matter spoken. Let us make sure that we glorify our wonderful Saviour in all we say.

1. See Appendix I, 'Clinical psychiatry and religion'.

9.
Has Rome changed?

One of the fantasies held most widely among evangelicals is that Rome has changed, and is as concerned for biblical evangelism as any of the leaders of so-called Protestant churches. Think of Pope John Paul's visit to Britain at Whitsuntide in 1982. Was not the present dynamic pope speaking constantly about the Lord Jesus Christ? Truth requires us to say immediately, 'Yes, he was.' But did you know that the following week, when he was among the Roman Catholic faithful in Portugal, he was constantly speaking about the Virgin Mary, and said very little about the Lord Jesus? Are we not entitled to conclude that his public relations officers did a really good job for him? Or at the very least, that he himself, who is no fool, was astute enough to know what would go down best wherever he was. I have read both lots of speeches with great care and find it difficult to draw any other conclusion. It would be wise to soft-pedal on the Virgin in England and to speak much of her Son; not so in Portugal.

An interesting feature of the pope's visit to Glasgow, for the celebration of the mass in front of many thousands of people, was the picture in a number of national newspapers at the time of a tree in Bellahouston Park. Under the picture was the caption: 'They've moved the tree.' For me this had a deeper significance than the editors intended! Our Saviour was once crucified on a tree, as the apostle Peter mentioned both in his great sermon on the Day of Pentecost and in his first letter (see 1 Peter 2:24). This was a once-for-all experience according to the Scriptures (see Hebrews 7:24-28; 9:24-28; 10:1-18, especially vv. 10-14). So any suggestion of a re-presentation of the offering of Christ on the cross is a highly significant 'moving of the tree'.

Too many of the British public have been taken in by the idea that the one unpardonable sin in the latter part of the twentieth century is intolerance. So we must not condemn Rome for believing differently about the Holy Communion service. 'If they like to call it the "mass", so be it! What harm is there in that?' So runs the thinking of many. We are told by many church leaders that we must not stir things up. We must stress the things we have in common. Doctrine divides; so we must play down the doctrines that we do not share. 'We will never win the attention of an indifferent world unless we get our act together!' Visible unity is essential, so we are told, to effective evangelism.

Our evangelical forebears used to think that the gulf between Anglicans and Roman Catholics was unbridgeable, but now we are assured that the Anglican-Roman Catholic Commission has nailed that bogeyman for ever. The published findings of this joint commission (ARCIC for short), warmly approved by the Anglican archbishops, show an amazing degree of harmony. Why? Not because Rome has changed, but because the Anglicans representing the established church have accepted the definitions offered by the Roman Catholic theologians as standing for what they stand for. Dr Runcie, now Lord Runcie, expressed himself very willing when he was Archbishop of Canterbury to come under the chairmanship of the pope in a united church. In his view there was nothing substantial that stood in the way of uniting with Rome as one church. What ARCIC said about the Eucharist, ministry and authority went for him.

Do the differences matter?

But is it true that the differences are minimal, so small that it is simply stupid to stay apart? Was it simply a matter of misunderstanding of each other's position that led to such a drastic separation at the time of the great Reformation? This is a fairly recent suggestion. But when we read the contemporary documents, we find each side so aware of the other's doctrinal position that the suggestion of mere misunderstanding can very quickly be ruled out of court. Rome's statements were not ambiguous. Her representatives spelled out very clearly what she believed. The Reformers were equally perspicuous in their statements. Each flatly contradicted the position of the other. It is sheer fantasy, or wishful thinking, to suggest that the division was only due to misunderstanding. There is a world of difference between righteousness *imputed* (put down to someone's account — the Protestant teaching) — and *imparted*, put into our hearts (the Catholic view).

The division was due to totally opposed teaching. Rome, strongly confirmed by the Council of Trent (1545-63), closed off all other options by stating categorically that 'Christ is truly, really and substantially contained in the sacrament under the appearance of sensible things [i.e. things that appear to be something to the senses]. By the consecration of the bread and wine a change is brought about of the whole substance of the bread into the body of Christ our Lord and of the whole substance of the wine into his blood. This change is called transubstantiation.' Vatican II (1962-1965) did not contradict this understanding of the sacrifice of the mass, or transubstantiation. 'Truly partaking of the body of the Lord in the breaking of the Eucharistic bread, we are taken up into communion with him and with one another.' And 'No Christian community ... can be built up unless it has its basis and centre in the celebration of the ... Eucharist.'[1]

The pope who called together his church leaders from all over the world, John XXIII, issued an encyclical, *Ad Petri Cathedram,* in which he came down very firmly on the side of the traditional doctrines of the mass and Mary, appealing to both Scripture and tradition. While he found a new name, 'separated brethren', for those formerly called heretics, he made it perfectly clear that reunion could only take place on the condition of returning to the true church and to the pope as the centre of unity.

John's successor as pope, Paul VI, was worried about all the Dutch priests who had begun to teach that the mass was a memorial feast. So he published *Mysterium Fidei,* an encyclical in which he strongly condemned the idea that the Holy Communion was only a memorial feast, and warned that anybody who taught this was heretical.

During two periods of convalescence I have had opportunity to watch Roman Catholic services on TV and have heard the faithful say, 'Lord, I am not worthy that thou shouldest come under my roof,' indicating clearly that they are expecting to receive the body and blood of Christ himself. The miraculous change to the elements of bread and wine is not soft-pedalled for the sake of impressing any Protestant observers. Transubstantiation is still the official teaching of the church of Rome. The progress of the ecumenical movement makes no difference to this.

When the British Council of Churches was formed, as a part of the World Council of Churches, Rome was prepared to send observers, but not to become a constituent member. She was very anxious to avoid the impression that she was just one among a number of churches each equally entitled to be known as a church. But with the passage of time, Rome rightly gained the impression that the other churches were weakening in their understanding of doctrine, and she has now emerged as the front-runner in the new Inter-Church Process, or Churches Together, as it is now called. Is this because she has changed? Not at all!

What Rome teaches today

Read what Rome's official teaching is today on how to become a Christian: 'Baptism is a sacrament which cleanses from original sin, makes us Christians, children of God, and members of the church.'

The same official document, a *Catechism of Christian doctrine*, published by the Catholic Truth Society in 1985 says,

> 'The Sacrament of the Holy Eucharist is the true Body and Blood of Jesus Christ, together with his soul and divinity under the appearance of bread and wine ... changed into the Body and Blood of Christ by the power of God, to whom nothing is impossible or difficult.'
>
> 'The blessed Eucharist is not a Sacrament only; it is also a sacrifice ... the offering of a victim by a priest to God alone... The Holy Mass is the sacrifice of the Body and Blood of Christ really present on the altar under the appearance of bread and wine, offered to God for the living and the dead.'

'The Holy Mass is one and the same sacrifice with that of the Cross, in as much as Christ who offered himself, a bleeding victim, on the cross to his heavenly Father, continues to offer himself in an unbloody manner on the altar, through the ministry of his priests.'

'The sacrifice of the Mass is offered for four ends:

'First to give supreme honour and glory to God;

'Secondly, to thank him for all his benefits;

'Thirdly, to satisfy God for our sins and to obtain the grace of repentance; and

'Fourthly, to obtain all other graces and blessing through Jesus Christ.

'The Mass is also a memorial of the passion and death of our Lord.'

Where Rome says 'also', those who take the Bible as their final authority say of the Holy Communion 'exclusively'. For the Scriptures teach with the greatest of clarity that Christ made one offering for sin, once and once only. He was himself the only sacrificial priest. He was himself the one victim, sacrificed by himself for sin.

As Hebrews 9:25-8 says, 'Nor did he enter heaven to offer himself [for sin] again and again... Then Christ would have had to suffer many times since the creation of the world. But now he has appeared once for all ... to do away with sin by the sacrifice of himself. Just as man is destined to die once, and after that to face judgement, so Christ was sacrificed once to take away the sins of many...'

Hebrews 10:10-14 is equally explicit: 'Day after day every priest stands ... again and again he offers the same sacrifices, which can never take away sins. But when this priest had offered for all time one sacrifice for sins, he sat down at the right hand of God. Since that time he waits for his enemies to be made his footstool, because by one sacrifice he has made perfect for ever those who are being made holy.'

The Book of Common Prayer Holy Communion Service has put it superbly in the words: 'Who made there, by his one oblation of himself once offered, a full, perfect, and sufficient sacrifice, satisfaction and oblation for our sins, and not for ours only, but for the whole world', that is, any sinner of any generation. This is what the Word of God says.

Why Roman errors are serious

Someone may ask, 'Is it worth making such a fuss about it? Does it matter that the church of Rome contradicts Scripture in this way?'

For those who take the Bible as their final authority for belief and behaviour it matters enormously. For what the Bible says, God says. And we cannot ride rough-shod over his Word without challenging his authority, putting ourselves and our tradition (since 1215 only!) above himself and his mind revealed in Scripture.

Belief in the mass is a serious error, for the mass is a robber! 'A robber!' you may say, 'that is a very serious allegation!' It is. Let me explain.

The mass robs *the Father* of the glory of having his Son once and for all as a single and sufficient sacrifice for sin, covering all believers who lived before Christ (Hebrews 10:1-9), all believers who have lived since Christ came to our rescue, and all who will believe in him before he comes as Judge of the living and of the dead.

It robs *the Son* of the glory of his finished work on the cross. In flat contradiction of the Scriptures it purports to drag him back into the place of a helpless sacrificial offering, instead of leaving him in glory at the Father's right hand. It is an offence to his divine majesty, while claiming to give God glory.

It robs *the Holy Spirit* of the glory of bearing unequivocal witness to the sufficiency and finality of that one offering once made.

The mass robs *the church* of the great focal point of its gospel, placing the hearer at the mercy of a 'sacrificing priest' to bring him near to God.

It robs *the believer* of his assurance. If Christ's sacrificial work is not yet ended, how can we be sure of the forgiveness of our sins? We are kept in a state of constant uncertainty, hope fighting against fear, instead of the biblical assurance that 'Therefore, there is now no condemnation for those who are in Christ Jesus,' and 'Neither death nor life … nor anything else in all creation, will be able to separate us from the love of God that is in Christ Jesus' (Romans 8:1,39).

The mass and a memorial feast are poles apart. But the differences are being played down in the interests of apparent church unity.

Rome has only changed in window dressing. She is more polite

to 'separated brethren', but her terms are unchanged: 'Come home!
The door is open.' Rome is more than willing to embrace all who
come to her — on her terms! Biblical realism flatly contradicts the
popular fantasy that Rome has changed in anything substantial or of
doctrinal importance. The teaching church will still tell the faithful
what to believe.

Recent pronouncements by leading Catholics

In case anyone should think Rome may have changed for the better
from a biblical point of view in the years since the Catechism printed
in 1985, let me quote from Father Tom Forrest, speaking at
Indianapolis 1990: 'My job, my role in evangelization is not just to
make Christians. Our job is to make people as richly and fully
Christian as we can make them by bringing them into the Catholic
Church... No, you don't just invite someone to be a Christian. You
invite them to come with you as a new parishioner of your Catholic
church. We don't just have the Eucharist as a symbol of the blood
and body of Christ; we drink the blood of Christ; Jesus is alive on
our altars, as offering and as a banquet of love.'

Tom Forrest was one of the main leaders at Brighton 91, where
Cardinal Basil Hume celebrated mass for the 800 Roman Catholic
delegates among the more than 2,500 delegates from all over the
world. This Eucharist was fully charismatic in form. Observers
present spoke of hands raised, embraces, repeated singing, 'singing
in the Spirit' and a first-person prophecy. But it was fully Catholic
in its content. For instance, Cardinal Hume said, 'We are one in
baptism,' and 'We're so lucky to have an official interpreter of the
Word of God — the teaching authority of the church.' You will
notice he did not say the official interpreter was the Holy Spirit, from
whom all believers have an anointing so that they may know the
truth for themselves.

The papal preacher to the pontifical household (might we call
him 'the domestic chaplain to the pope'?) spoke at Brighton on 'our
unity in Christ': 'Ecumenism based on love can be realized now. We
must be concerned about truth in the right place, but we can advance
in love now... The message is not written or proclaimed, but lived
— love.' He gave no consideration to the question of how love is

related to truth. In summarizing his impressions, one observer said, 'It is difficult to resist the conclusion that such unity as there was came from shared forms of experience and "worship", rather than from shared truth. The Bible did not figure significantly in the proceedings. All the varied views seemed to assume that they already knew what the Bible said, so they saw no need constantly to hear it.' The new traditions seem to be replacing the old truths at a fair rate of knots for 'Protestants' present at this widely publicized 'consultation', when beside the large contingent of Roman Catholic delegates there were no less than 750 Anglican delegates present, and some 1,000 nonconformists, all charismatic.

A note of caution

There is a note of caution to be added to this chapter. Whereas we have lived to see the vast Soviet Empire go back on the Communist orthodoxy of Marx and Lenin, we are not likely to see the church of Rome going back on the doctrines taught as things which must be believed if one is to be saved. But what many of us are seeing is the emerging of many brought up as orthodox Catholics who no longer believe in the 'miracle' of transubstantiation and who seem to have been born again through the reading of the unannotated Word of God. Habit dies hard and if their families are faithfully attending the weekly celebration of the mass, they find it extremely hard to break away. So there they go, with other members of their families, to observe something they no longer believe is a valid expression of New Testament faith.

We should be praying that the number of these folk will grow, and that they will have the courage to break out of their traditional ecclesiastical framework and find their way to a church that takes the Bible for its final authority in all matters of belief and behaviour. In the meantime, how should we view them? If they are truly born again, we must view them as brothers and sisters in Christ, 'pilgrims together' indeed. In many respects, such people are 'good Christians', but in those very same respects, they are bad Catholics!

May the God of all grace, who led Luther, Calvin and Zwingli on the Continent, Bilney, Latimer and Cranmer in England, and many thousands more, out of Rome in the great sixteenth-century

Reformation and revival, do the same with many thousands in our generation. And that in spite of 'evangelical' leaders who have declared in recent years that they have come to regard that Reformation as a great mistake, if not a terrible tragedy!

1. Quoted by Robert Ives in the *Dictionary of the Christian Church*, Paternoster Press

10.
Who is the church for?

It was Archbishop Temple who first said, 'The church is the only society which exists for the benefit of non-members.' I wonder how many times you have heard that pronouncement made in different churches? It sounds very impressive the first time you hear it, and if you have anything like a heart for evangelism, you cannot help feeling there is something very attractive about the memorable way it is put. I can still remember the first time I heard it. I thought, 'What a challenging statement!' Next time, it was, 'There it goes again. How interesting!' Then I began to wonder, 'How much truth is there in this?' After that I reflected on the New Testament teaching about the church and began to realize it was not only somewhat misleading, in so far as it presents a half-truth as if it were the whole truth, but it can also be dangerous.

The chief danger is that it can replace the central person in the whole New Testament concept of the church by a person on the fringe, or even further away. It also runs counter to church history as written in the New Testament and seems to ride roughshod over some of the very clear statements about the church found in the New Testament. In fact it seems to cancel out the main thrust of the Greek word for church! *'Ekklesia'* means 'called out'. The church consists of a people who have been called out. And while they may be called out partly in order to be sent into the world, they are, first and foremost, called out to a person, given by the Father to his Son that they might be his special people. 'This people have I formed for myself; they shall show forth my praise' (Isaiah 43:21, AV) may have referred primarily to God's Old Testament people, the Jews. But when we come to Peter's first letter in the New Testament we find believers in Christ called out of darkness from all over the world. They form a people who once were not a people, but are now the people of God' (1 Peter 2:9-10). Then, having received mercy from God, the same people are appealed to, or urged, 'as aliens and strangers in the world, to abstain from sinful desires, which war against your soul. Live such good lives among the pagans that, though they accuse you of doing wrong, they may see your good deeds and glorify God on the day he visits us.' How are we to understand that day? Is Peter talking of a day when the non-members will become members in a big way, or of the coming Day of Judgement, when the secrets of unbelieving hearts are laid bare? Sad to say, I think a better case can be made out for the latter.

Now in the Word of God we find various metaphors used to describe the church of Jesus Christ. The church is Christ's body, Christ's bride, Christ's fulness or *pleroma*, God's family, God's building, God's field, God's heirs, God's children, God's flock, children of light, the pillar and ground of truth and God's stars shining in a dark world. We need to look at these pictures one by one if we are to grasp at least something of what God means the church to be.

New Testament pictures of the church

The church is the body of Christ

'Just as each of us has one body with many members, and these members do not all have the same function, so in Christ we who are many form one body, and each member belongs to all the others' (Romans 12:4-5). 'Now you are the body of Christ, and each one of you is a part of it' (1 Corinthians 12:27). 'God placed all things under [Christ's] feet and appointed him to be head over everything for the church, which is his body...' (Ephesians 1:22).

When we are physically and mentally in good health, our bodies express fairly accurately the wishes of our head, brain, or mind. When we are ill, the body may start doing its own thing — acting in ways that our minds do not consciously approve of. Parkinson's Disease is a vivid example of this. The hands of the patient do their own thing, apart from strong medication, no matter how hard the mind tries to keep them still. There seems to be far too much evidence of a 'spiritual Parkinson's Disease' among many who call themselves Christians. If we are not reading our Bibles daily we are doing our own thing in any Christian activity we are engaged in. The same is true if we are not praying regularly in a humble, submissive way, wanting only God's will to be done.

Some are hyper-active in outreach, and never spend long enough quietly in the presence of the risen Lord to 'recharge their batteries', as it were. Others are hyper-active in 'praise' and what they term 'worship', and seem blissfully unaware of the needs of lost sinners all around them. We cannot reach them all, but the Lord does want us to reach some in his name! Some are bogged down in organizational responsibilities that seem to have no relevance whatsoever to the spread of the gospel. We need to ask ourselves, are our weekly activities really necessary, or are we just keeping a fruitless machine ticking over? How we need to pray for wisdom!

Church members in New Testament times went off the rails in all sorts of directions. You have only to think of Corinth! God is looking for balanced Christians, feeding on his Word, responding in honest prayer to what they read, remembering Christ's death, remembering the needs of his servants at home and overseas, training younger Christians, reaching out to non-Christians and always on the look-out for God at work in prepared souls (John 10:16).

Christ, the Head of the church, which is his body, wants every member of his body to live a spiritually healthy life. We have all heard the saying, 'All work and no play makes Jack a dull boy.' In other words, Jack is not living a balanced life. To parody that, we can say in Christian terms, 'All outreach and no teaching makes Jack a thin sort of Christian! All outreach and no worship makes Jack a poor disciple, low on spiritual calories and getting more and more empty.' And all worship or teaching and no links with perishing sinners — 'those who are without', as the AV describes the unsaved — and Jack is nowhere near functioning in a healthy way as a true disciple of the Lord Jesus. Not that we can all be good at everything Christians do! To every man his gift; to every man his work! (Mark 13:34). But we must be at the disposal of our Head each day, or our sickness will show, and we will drag our fellow-believers back, instead of helping the whole body forward and honouring our Head.

The church is the bride of Christ

'Christ loved the church and gave himself up for her to make her holy, cleansing her by the washing with water through the word, and to present her to himself as a radiant church [bride], without stain or wrinkle or any other blemish, but holy and blameless...' Christ loves, feeds and cares for the church (Ephesians 5:23-29). When we meet as his congregation we should be quick to thank him for his constant love and care.

The church is Christ's fulness

'The church ... is ... the fulness of him who fills everything in every way' (Ephesians 1:22-23). The word 'fulness' conveys an immediate picture. All that I am lacking is to be found in him. Take him away from what we call 'Christian' and everything is hopelessly empty. Emptiness is the opposite of fulness. All that I need is in the Lord Jesus. He satisfies the longing soul. I am most stupid if I do not come constantly to him for all my deepest needs to be met, and all my daily activities to be covered. I must also tell him I am at his disposal for all his purposes of grace to be worked out in me.

To a sailor the word 'fulness' would convey another picture. The Greeks used it to describe the crew of a ship. We are to obey our Captain's orders, or we are as bad as mutineers, and we shall hinder his purposes and timetable. Let us be where he wants us to be! Let us go where he wants us to go!

The church is God's family

'You are all sons of God through faith in Christ Jesus ... clothed ... with Christ... There is neither Jew nor Greek ... you are all one in Christ Jesus. If you belong to Christ, then you are Abraham's seed, and heirs according to the promise' of God to Abraham about the worldwide extent of his family — God's family (Galatians 3:26-29). What a wonderful privilege to belong to such a family!

The church is God's building, Christ's building, a holy temple

'On this rock I will build my church ...' (Matthew 16:18). 'And the Lord added to their number [the church] daily those who were being saved' (Acts 2:47). 'You are members of God's household, built on the foundation of the apostles and prophets, with Christ Jesus himself as the chief cornerstone. In him the whole building is joined together and rises to become a holy temple in the Lord. And in him you too are being built together to become a dwelling in which God lives by his Spirit' (Ephesians 2:19-22). Note the tenses!

The church is God's field

'What ... is Apollos? And what is Paul? Only servants, through whom you came to believe — as the Lord has assigned to each his task. I planted the seed, Apollos watered it, but God made it grow. So neither he who plants nor he who waters is anything, but only God, who makes things grow. The man who plants and the man who waters have one purpose, and each will be rewarded according to his own labour. For we are God's fellow-workers; you are God's field, God's building' (1 Corinthians 3:5-9).

The church contains God's heirs

'Now if we are children, then we are heirs — heirs of God and co-heirs with Christ' (Romans 8:17). '[God] saved us ... because of his mercy. He saved us ... through Jesus Christ our Saviour, so that, having been justified by his grace, we might become heirs having the hope of eternal life' in his presence (Titus 3:5-7).

The church is made up of children of God

In heaven they will 'neither marry nor be given in marriage, and they can no longer die; for they are like the angels. They are God's children, since they are children of the resurrection... He is not the God of the dead, but of the living, for to him all are alive' (Luke 20:35-38). Let us try to take in the implications of that. Our believing dead are only dead to us. To him they are gloriously alive, more alive than ever they were on earth.

'Because you are sons, God sent the Spirit of his Son into our hearts, the Spirit who calls out, "Abba, Father" ... and since you are a son, God has made you also an heir' (Galatians 4:6-7). What an inheritance we who believe are coming into — but we have not yet entered into it!

The church is God's flock

'I have other sheep that are not of this [Jewish] sheep pen. I must
bring them also. They too will listen to my voice, and there shall be
one flock and one shepherd' (John 10:16). 'Feed my sheep' (John
21:17). 'Be shepherds of God's flock that is under your care' (1 Peter
5:2). The flock needs feeding, not just training to be shepherds.

The church is composed of children of light

'The people of this world are more shrewd in dealing with their own
kind than are the people of the light. I tell you,' says the Saviour, 'use
worldly wealth [cash, books, time, hospitality] to gain friends for
yourself, so that when it is gone, you will be welcomed into eternal
dwellings' (Luke 16:8-9). Who will be in our welcome party? 'Put
your trust in the light while you have it, so that you may become sons
of light' (John 12:36).

The church is the pillar and ground of truth

'I am writing you these instructions,' says Paul, 'so that ... you will
know how people ought to conduct themselves in God's household,
which is the church of the living God, the pillar and foundation
[think of a candlestick] of the truth.' And what is the truth that must
be held high? What is the candle that is to shine forth? It is none other
than the 'mystery of godliness', namely that the Son of God has
appeared in a human body, 'was vindicated by the Spirit' at his
resurrection, 'was seen by angels' (at his resurrection as well as at
his birth!) was preached among the nations, was believed on in the
world, was taken up in glory' (1 Timothy 3:14-16). Christ, not
personal fulfilment, is our gospel!
    One aspect of the church is seen in God's children *shining like
stars*. What is the church here for? To 'do everything without
complaining or arguing, so that you may become blameless and
pure, children of God without fault in a crooked and depraved
generation, in which you shine like stars in the universe as you hold
out the word of life' (Philippians 2:14-16). Here we have the church
reaching out to a dark, dark world. But it is only one important
function among many, if we are to do justice to the other word
pictures.

The purpose of the church

Should we not, without for one moment watering down enthusiasm for evangelism or outreach, recognize that the church exists primarily for the pleasure of God the Father, for the glory of God the Son and the expression of his wishes, and is to be the vehicle for the fulfilment of the active purposes of God the Holy Spirit?

In other words, the main *raison d'être* of the church is not the benefit of the non-member, 'the good of the rank outsider,' but the glory of God, who has gathered it out of the world at such cost to himself. That old saying from the Scottish Catechism, 'Man's chief end is to glorify God and to enjoy him for ever,' sums it up well.

For some this seems to have been altered to read: 'The believing person's chief aim is to join with others in reaching out to the unsaved, to bring all kinds of benefits to them, spiritual and material.' This makes me ask the question: 'Has one of the motivations which should spur the church on been blown up out of all proportion to replace the other basic motivations in the thinking of some keen evangelicals?' We are here first and foremost for God. The very first Christians continued steadfastly in the apostles' doctrine or teaching, and in their fellowship, in the breaking of bread in remembrance of Christ's death for them and in prayers. From Acts 2:42 we may draw the conclusion that their top priorities included: being taught, in public and in private; having fellowship, in small numbers and large; meeting the Lord at his table 'in remembrance of him'; praying the prayers they had learned as children, which they were always hearing in the synagogue or temple or at home. And because they stayed close to the Lord and one another, there was a magnetism about them which God used to alert others to the truth as it is in Jesus, and drew others into their fellowship. 1 Corinthians 14:24-25 illustrates this principle. Love is attractive, and the combination of love and light is most effective for the enlarging of the boundaries of the kingdom of God.

When we consider that only three out of twelve pictures of the church found in the New Testament point clearly to outreach — God's stars, children of light and the pillar and ground of truth — we should be careful not to go overboard for the thesis that 'The church is the only society which exists for the benefit of non-members.'

A scriptural basis for evangelism

This sentence is no doubt uttered with the best of motives, namely to stir up believers to face their responsibilities to the unsaved. But that can surely be done on the basis of scriptural examples. We shall examine a few of them.

1. The Great Commission. The disciples were commanded to go into all the world and preach the good news, 'and make disciples of [men and women from] all nations, baptizing them in the name of the Father, and of the Son and the Holy Spirit and teaching them to obey everything I have commanded you. And surely I am with you always, to the very end of the age' (Matthew 28:19-20). Those first disciples are not here today, but the commission holds good to the end of the age, and so does the promise of his presence. These words of challenge are binding on us, as on all Christians till the end of the age, that is, till he comes to gather the rest of his harvest home.

2. Words of great comfort. We read that the Lord 'had to go [AV, "must needs go"] through Samaria' (John 4:4). Why? Because 'The Son of Man came to seek and to save what was lost' (Luke 19:10).

3. The great example of the early Christians from Jerusalem. Scattered abroad as a result of persecution, they did not think first and foremost of their own safety, but passed on the good news wherever they went (Acts 8:4).

4. The great objective of the apostle to the Gentiles, to speak so effectively about Christ and sin and forgiveness and the need of repentance and faith that people turn to the Lord (Acts 26:18-20).

5. The great compassion Paul felt. His heart's desire and his prayer to God for his nation was that people might be saved (Romans 10:1). May God grant us similar compassion for the lost.

6. The great concern of the Father in heaven. Peter tells us that 'The Lord ... is patient ... not wanting anyone to perish, but everyone to come to repentance' (2 Peter 3:9).

I have dealt with the subject of personal evangelism in *How to share your faith*, (which is also published by Evangelical Press) so I am not going to repeat that material here, but I recommend anyone who wants to know more about it to obtain a copy of that book. Would to God that all the Lord's people were alive to their responsibility to pass on the good news about the Lord Jesus, and the opportunities that are all around us for doing this!

A summary

Having said that, let me sum up what I find in the New Testament about the purpose of the church.

The church exists primarily for:
1. The glory of God the Father. It is his idea.
2. The glory of God the Son. It is his bride.
3. The glory of God the Holy Spirit. It is his temple.
4. The benefit of new believers, who need to be nurtured, taught and integrated in worship and obedience.
5. The benefit of older believers, who are to be taught, trained (discipled), encouraged and warned. It is their school and hospital.
6. The benefit of mature believers, who need to be constantly reminded of the great truths of our faith and to have their hearts continually warmed. The more we give, the more we keep! It is their spiritual home.
7. The benefit of non-members, those not yet saved. It is the believers' springboard.

Some are saying these days that church only exists for the outsider, and everything must be trimmed to focus on him and centre on where he is at. Others think the young are the only people that really matter. The older ones have had their chance! The young are the church of the future! Christ, not the outsider, nor the youth, is to be the focal point of the Christian's life and worship and witness. 'To me, to live is Christ!'

In a hospital consulting room I saw a lamp used for close examinations. It was made up of eighty sections or slivers of mirror. Each section was highly polished. All were rightly related to the source of light. Each played its part. If one sliver had been broken or dirty it would have stood out. As it was, all were clean. This picture stirred up a great longing in my heart, for clean church members, rightly related to the light himself, and to one another.

11.
Do all roads lead to God?

Has a ruler the right to make clear the right way to approach him? We have only to ask the question to realize that the correct answer is, 'Of course!' Then how much more has God, the King of kings and the Lord of lords, the right to indicate the way to approach him and to insist on people coming that way, or else being excluded from his presence? But there are many in so-called Christian circles who look on such a statement as rather naïve, if not incredibly bigoted.

Some will remember the lecture given by Dr (now Lord) Runcie in Lambeth Palace in 1986 on 'Christianity and World Religions'. He was then Archbishop of Canterbury. He said we should 'recognize that other faiths than our own are genuine mansions of the Spirit with many rooms to be discovered, rather than solitary fortresses to be attacked... All the centuries that the Spirit of God has been working in Christians, he must also have been working in Hindus, Buddhists, Muslims and others ... we must learn to recognize the work of the Spirit at the centre of each of our faiths.'

He went on to say that before his visit to India, 'There were certainties of an encapsulated Western Christianity,' whereas after the visit, 'There were new ways of thinking about God, Christ, and the world... Encounter with other faiths can deepen and enrich us... There is a certain incompleteness in each of our traditions... Ultimately all religions possess a provisional, interim character as ways and signs to help us in our pilgrimage to ultimate truth and perfection... We will have to abandon any narrowly conceived

Christian apologetics based on a sense of superiority and on exclusive claims to truth.'

Two years later, in April 1988, at a forum of spiritual and parliamentary leaders, Dr Runcie said, 'We must recognize the 'divine spark' in all human beings, and that 'The unity of human beings is grounded and crowned as an ultimate reality which is greater than the recognition of it in each of our traditions.'

But is this the Christianity of the New Testament? Is it not syncretism at the highest level in the land? It is true that he also said, 'For my part, I am bound to say as a Christian that definitive apprehension of the divine occurs in an encounter with Jesus Christ.' But in saying this, was Dr Runcie implying anything more than that Christianity is the best way, and a perfectly valid way, even if incomplete, for Christians? Is he not also teaching that we must not dream of claiming that Christianity is unique, and the only way for sinners to approach a holy God?

What encouragement is there here for missionaries trying to win people of other faiths to allegiance to the Lord Jesus Christ? What help is there for those in Britain seeking to lead to faith in Christ some of the many key people from other lands who are studying for a while in our academic establishments? What would a Philip trained in the thinking of Dr Runcie have had to say to an Ethiopian top official whom he met on his way home from Jerusalem? Could it have been anything more than, 'Let us share our different insights into religious truth. I don't feel it is my duty to try to convert you to my faith'?[1]

The New Testament view

When we turn to the New Testament, what a different approach confronts us! In Acts 4:10-12 we find the apostle Peter saying, after the healing of a blind beggar at the gate called Beautiful, 'Know this, you and all the people of Israel: It is by the name of Jesus Christ of Nazareth, whom you crucified but whom God raised from the dead, that this man stands before you healed. He is "the stone you builders rejected, which has become the capstone". Salvation is found in no one else, for there is no other name under heaven given to men by which we must be saved.'

Someone may say, 'Impulsive Peter — bigoted as they come! Typical! The disciple stepping far ahead of his gentle Master!' But wait a minute! Was Peter really going beyond the claims his Master made for himself? Listen to these words spoken by the Lord himself in reply to the question put to him by the apostle Thomas: '"Lord, we don't know where you are going, so how can we know the way?" Jesus answered, "I am the way and the truth and the life. No one comes to the Father except through me."' The Greek text is even more emphatic than the English. He uses the personal pronoun 'I', instead of the 'I' just being included in the form of the verb, as is usual in Greek. So it could be translated, 'I, and I alone, am the way … to the Father.' And that includes the Father's house with its ample room (v. 2). This is surely the most positive and exclusive claim. And in case we don't grasp its exclusiveness, what the Saviour has put so positively, he then proceeds to put equally exclusively in a negative way: 'No one comes to the Father except through me.'

So the quarrel of the syncretists, who see all religions as having some essential insight that we all need, whatever tradition we were brought up in, is not with Peter after all. It is with the Lord Jesus Christ himself — not the Christ of soft modern thinking, but the Christ of the Scriptures.

Peter is not alone among the apostles in taking a leaf out of his Master's book. Listen to Paul writing to the Romans: 'Paul, a servant of Christ Jesus, called to be an apostle and set apart for the gospel of God — the gospel he promised beforehand through his prophets in the Holy Scriptures regarding his Son … Jesus Christ our Lord. Through him and for his name's sake, we received grace and apostleship to call people from among all the Gentiles to the obedience that comes from faith … I am not ashamed of the gospel, because it is the power of God for the salvation of everyone who believes: first for the Jew, then for the Gentile' (Romans 1:1-5,16).

This gospel is for all the world, because the whole world is held accountable to God, and in his sight all are sinners, needing to be saved by the one and only Saviour, God's dear Son (Romans 3:19; 4:9; 5:8).

Paul makes it abundantly clear that according to New Testament thinking, Jews are not to be looked on as saved just because they are Jews. Otherwise he would not dream of saying, 'Brothers, my heart's desire and prayer to God for the Israelites is that they may be saved.' What? Is he saying that those who received a divine revelation through God's great servant Moses are not saved? Yes, that is exactly what he is saying. Zeal is not enough. The law of God is not enough. Trying to keep it is not enough. All men need a Saviour: someone to do for them what they cannot do for themselves — not even the best of them at their best moments. Jesus Christ, the Son of God is that Saviour, he and no one else.

We don't have to bring about the incarnation, bringing Christ down from heaven. God has seen to that. We don't have to organize the resurrection. God has seen to that. What then do we have to do? 'If you confess with your mouth, "Jesus is Lord," [not Caesar, but Jesus!] and believe in your heart that God raised him from the dead, you will be saved. For it is with your heart that you believe and are justified, and it is with your mouth that you confess and are saved. As the Scripture says, "Anyone who trusts in him will never be put to shame."'

This is true for 'anyone', whatever our race, or place, IQ, or upbringing, and whatever tradition we were brought up in. Could it be clearer? Paul goes on to underline this: 'For there is no difference between Jew and Gentile — the same Lord is Lord of all and richly blesses all who call on him, for, "Everyone who calls on the name of the Lord will be saved." How, then, can they call on the one they have not believed in? And how can they believe in the one of whom they have not heard? And how can they hear without someone preaching to them? And how can they preach unless they are sent? As it is written, "How beautiful are the feet of those who bring good news!" ... faith comes from hearing the message, and the message is heard through the word of Christ' (Romans 10:1-17).

Paul speaks in the next verse of the good news going to the ends of the world. Why? Is it simply a matter of universal need, and the gospel being the one and only answer to that universal need? No, though that is true. It goes back further than that. We find the roots of this clear thinking in what we call 'the Great Commission'. Speaking to the eleven disciples in Galilee, the risen Lord tells them, 'All authority in heaven and on earth has been given to me. Therefore go and make disciples of all nations, baptizing them in the name of the Father and of the Son and of the Holy Spirit, and teaching them to obey everything I have commanded you. And surely I am with you always, to the very end of the age.'

From these solemn words we should note three things of great significance. Firstly, the authority he was given extends to heaven and *all* the earth. It was not to be shared with a Buddha who lived on earth before him, or a Muhammad who would be born some seven hundred years later. Secondly, the 'them' in the phrase 'baptizing them' is masculine in Greek, indicating it is disciples, not nations, who are to be baptized, since the Greek word for nations is neuter, not masculine. Last, but not least, these terms of reference are valid for all generations, which includes ours, until the very end of the age. Two promises are tucked away inside these words: there are going to be preachers of Christ's gospel to the end of time, and they are going to win disciples up to the very end of the age. What encouragement for Christians! As David Livingstone said in his memorable phrase, 'These are the words of a perfect gentleman.' He will surely keep his word.

How is Christianity unique?

Some Christians are more influenced than they ought to be by people with big names. So when an archbishop says something that seems to make sense from a sociological point of view, they may be a bit shaken, and instead of asking, 'What do the Scriptures say?' they may ask, 'Can I justify what I have always believed when such a highly-placed and clever man says my position is no longer tenable?' Dr Runcie has indicated that while Christianity is his preferred way of approaching God, he no longer regards it as unique. To those who believe the Bible is their final authority for all matters of belief and practice, a Christianity that is not unique is not the Christianity they recognize. But the reader is fully entitled to ask, 'In what ways is Christianity unique?' So let me spell out five aspects in which Christianity is unique.

Firstly, Christianity is the only faith in the world which offers the individual *a direct personal relationship* with the holy, sinless, founder of the faith.

Secondly, Christianity is the only faith in the world which offers *the forgiveness of sins at the expense of the founder* of the faith.

Thirdly, Christianity is the only faith in the world which offers *eternal life as a free gift now*, through the grace of the founder of the faith.

Fourthly, Christianity is the only faith in the world which allows you to bring nothing, nothing but your sins. *Salvation is entirely undeserved.*

Nothing in my hand I bring,
Simply to the cross I cling;
Naked, come to thee for dress,
Helpless, look to thee for grace.

Christianity alone satisfies God's justice, and humbles us so that we have to come to God on God's terms, or not at all!

Finally, Christianity alone clearly shows *the futility of standing on tiptoe trying to reach up to God.* Christianity is God in his loving-kindness and sheer mercy reaching down to us in our guilt and need (see Ephesians 2:8-10 and Titus 3:3-7).

Someone may be thinking, 'What does he know about other religions? All his arguments seem to be built up from the Bible. Is it true that no other religion, not even the New Age, offers these things? After a careful reading of the holy books of other religions and discussions with devoted pundits of other faiths, I have yet to find any faith that can come anywhere near these distinctives of Christianity.[2]

Christians don't just claim to have information that is interesting for those with religious inclinations. They are under an obligation to confront, however gently, their contemporaries with the person in whom their faith is focused. Christians declare that God has revealed himself fully and decisively in Christ. And that Christ is absolutely inescapable. We either meet him as our Saviour on earth, or we face him as our Judge after death. So Christians insist that God calls us to repent, to do a U-turn, to turn right round from living life our own way, to believe in, put our trust in, the Lord Jesus Christ. It is not enough to believe the right things about him. We must commit ourselves personally to him, seeking from now on to serve the living God with heart and mind and soul and strength. He is so worthy of our total allegiance and daily adoration and worship. To God be all the glory for ever and ever! Amen.

1. It is evident that I am not alone in expressing deep concern about this issue. I was heartened to read a heading running right across a page of a

national newspaper on Friday, 6 December 1991 which said, 'Clergy defy Carey on multi-faith service.' An extract from this article is reproduced in Appendix 3.

2. I have summarized the essentials of most of the faiths we are likely to come across in a booklet entitled, *Christianity — just another religion?* published by Victory Booklets, but for a fuller treatment I would urge you to read Sir Norman Anderson's books published by the Inter-Varsity Press, and *Some Modern Faiths* and *The Challenge of the Cults* by Maurice Burrell and J. Stafford Wright.

Appendix I:
The centrality of the cross

The following words come from the pen of Group Captain Alfred Knowles, OBE, AFC. He planned to give them as a devotional talk at his last council meeting of the Soldiers' and Airmen's Scripture Readers' Association on 8 May 1991, when he was due to hand over the chairmanship to Brigadier Ian Dobbie, but the Lord called his faithful servant home five days before that.

More than a symbol

The cross is the recognized symbol of the Christian faith, but of much greater importance is its significance as the centre and crux of the gospel. St Saviour's Church, Guildford, has a spire surmounted by a cross. A recent survey showed the cross was loose in its socket as the stonework had deteriorated. The remedy was to fix an extension to the vertical member of the cross, drill a hole down through the stonework and secure the cross from inside the steeple. Happy is the church or organization which has the cross held securely in the heart of its membership!

Some years ago I heard of a young man preparing for the ministry. He sought the advice of an older minister whom he respected. He was told to learn by heart 1 Corinthians chapter 1 verse 18 to chapter 2 verse 2, and to repeat it to himself every morning as he shaved. This passage starts with: 'The preaching of the cross is to those who perish fooolishness; but to us who are saved it is the power of God,' and it ends with Paul's affirmation: 'For I am determined not to know anything among you save Jesus Christ, and him crucified.'

Old yet ever new

There is a great need at this time to stress the message of the cross. Its unique importance has been neglected as the church and some of its leaders have emphasized other aspects of the gospel, often at the expense of the cross. As one young man said to me when I had talked about the message of the cross, 'That's old hat.' Yes, it is old. In fact it was in the mind of God from the foundation of the world, but the significance of the cross will never grow old or become out of date as long as man is in his unredeemed state. And even in glory, when our redemption is complete, we will still be singing about it (see Revelation chapter 5). Let us see to it that the focus of our witness is Christ Jesus and him crucified. In the cross we have the supreme expression of God's love for sinful men and women, the sure foundation of our salvation, and the pattern and power of our life for him.

Alfred Knowles did not it was to be his final message. He could not have sent a more timely message if he had known he was on the brink of eternity. 'He being dead yet speaketh!'

Appendix II:
Clinical psychiatry and religion

The following is an extract from a review by Dr Douglas Johnson.

International Psychiatric Clinics — Vol. 5, No. 4, edited by E. Mansell Patterson, Boston, Littlebrown & Company, 1969, 328 pages.

This is primarily a book — as its title implies — for psychiatrists. Part 2 has a section entitled 'Glossolalia — a mystical experience'. If the experimental work and the sampling were both soundly based and large enough, the work and the conclusions could be important at this juncture in church history.

The paper provides a brief sketch of the phenomenon of 'speaking in tongues' in the Western Christian tradition, as well as in other religions, such as those of India and China. Of most immediate relevance are the views of the authors concerning the socio-cultural distribution, the personality and psycho-pathology of the 'glossolalist', the mechanisms of psycho-linguistics and of intrapsychic states. The chief interest must centre in the experimental findings from work done in connection with a group of volunteers, some of whom were students. If these studies can be accepted as scientifically reliable and valid, then the conclusions of the workers have considerable significance for our understanding of the contemporary phenomenon of 'speaking in tongues'.

Amongst a number of conclusions stated by the authors are:

1. 'Glossolalia is a learnt phenomenon and can be reproduced by naïve experimental subjects either by imitation or
upon request to "make up a strange language".'
2. 'Linguistic analyses among English-speakers reveal
that glossolalia is composed of basic English phonemes, but
employs a restricted linguistic code.'
3. 'Using associating techniques glossolalia can be
shown to have emotional meaning to subjects.'
4. It 'can be divided into two types: playful and serious ...
reflecting different intra-psychic functions'.
5. It 'represents a border-line phenomenon in the tran-
sition from inner private thought-speech to external objective
language'.
6. 'Often in glossolalia the "feeling tone" part of inner
speech is transposed on to automatic, externalized phonemic
sequences, thereby allowing the individual to express feeling
and emotion without revealing their manifest content.'
Perhaps the most relevant conclusion is: 'In the cases of
students whom we studied, we were struck by the lack of
regression of ego functions that occurred. These students
were able to launch wilfully into glossolalia with little change
of consciousness or associated ego functions. Here we observe what might be termed a highly "focal regression" in the
service of the ego... The glossolalic knows his "tongue" well,
that is, it is a familiar object to him. Because of this and his
perception that it brings him closer to God, his "tongue" gives
him security when he needs it.'...

Whatever else the modern phenomenon is (and even if it be
granted that it is God-given), it is something other than what the
writer in Acts 2 was describing on the Day of Pentecost.

Appendix III:
Clergy oppose multi-faith services

The following article, by Damian Thompson, appeared in the Daily Telegraph *on Friday, 6 December 1991, under the heading 'Clergy defy Carey on multi-faith service'.*

Two thousand Anglican clergy have defied the Archbishop of Canterbury by signing an open letter published today, calling for an end to the annual multi-faith service in Westminster Abbey... In the largest protest of its kind in the [Anglican] church's history, a fifth of all the serving clergy say the service and events like it 'conflict with the Christian duty to proclaim the gospel'.

By signing the letter, they have gone against the advice of Dr George Carey, who accused its authors of 'playing on Christian fears about encounter with other faiths' and asked them to abandon the project.

The letter ... is the product of an unusual alliance between the leaders of the General Synod's Anglo-Catholic and evangelical lobbies. The signatories, who include the Ven. George Austin, Archdeacon of York, and Canon Michael Saward of St Paul's Cathedral, say they are 'deeply concerned' by inter-faith gatherings involving Christians. 'We believe these events, however motivated, conflict with the Christian duty to proclaim the gospel.

'They imply that salvation is offered by God not only through Jesus Christ but by other means, and thus deny his uniqueness and finality as the only Saviour', the letter says.

'These events are frequently deeply hurtful to those in this country who have come from other religions into the Christian faith and also to Christian minorities in other lands, both of whom have frequently experienced persecution from the other faiths, especially where such faiths are unwilling to tolerate conversions or the existence of minority Christian communities.'

Should we not thank God for those who have had the courage to stand up and be counted for their faithfulness to the New Testament teaching and their ordination vows?

Synopsis

It may help some readers to have a brief summary of the argument or contents of each chapter:

1. Is Scripture enough?

The Bible is in danger of being relegated to a secondary place in the lives of some who would call themselves 'evangelical'. They believe God's Word comes to them today primarily through the hot-line of 'prophecies' from someone who is an open channel for the mind of God. Certainly, their teachers say such prophetic words must always be checked to see if they contradict Scripture at any point, for no word from God would contradict Scripture. But the relegation of Scripture in this setting to a checking function not only downgrades Scripture as being insufficient for the revelation of God's will to today's Christians, but is to my mind an 'evangelical fantasy'.

2. What is the heart of the gospel?

Is it the cross of our Saviour? Or is it the outpouring of the Spirit at Pentecost? We are often told that the modern mind is not concerned about guilt when it is personal rather than structural (i.e. the guilt of the individual as opposed to that of society at large or of big business or other institutions) and that modern man is more interested in power than in pardon. However, is it not part of the Christian teacher's duty to teach people the questions they ought to be asking, rather than to try to answer the questions they, in their spiritual blindness, think to be of paramount importance?

3. What are the new wineskins?

Do we all need to leave our long-established churches and come under the new management of those who are called 'apostles' in their own circles? On the other hand, are all 'churches' worthy of being kept at all costs?

4. What are the 'greater works' of John 14:12?

Is God expecting the church leaders of today to do greater works than the Saviour did? If so, what are they? Did the Saviour mean, as some teach, simply 'more numerous works of the same kind' that he himself and the apostles did? Or is there another biblical explanation of this phrase?

5. What about healing on demand?

Is divine healing for all, and for everything, if only we will claim it? Or is there a parallel to the verses in Hebrews 11:34,37, where we read of some who 'escaped the edge of the sword' by faith, while others were 'put to death by the sword'? The Greek text indicates it was the same sort of sword, the same sort of faith and the very same God. Is divine healing a matter of God's sovereignty rather than of man's faith and importunity?

6. Can we claim prosperity for all?

Is the famous Korean pastor, Paul Yonggi-cho, right when he gives prosperity such a high priority in his teaching about what believers should be expecting? Is to 'name it and claim it' consistent with what the Bible teaches about the social status of believers? Are we poor only if we fail to take God's Word seriously? Are Kenneth and Gloria Copeland right in their prosperity teaching, which has attracted thousands in Britain? Surely this one and the same teaching has a natural attraction for all of us! We could all do with a bit more money! But what do the Scriptures say about the believer and money and prosperity?

7. *What do we mean by the baptism and fulness of the Spirit?*

Should all Christians be seeking a second experience of grace which brings them power for service, powerful living and transforms mediocrity into an exhilarating experience of useful Christianity? Is our greatest weakness failure to enter into this experience, failure to hang on desperately till God grants it to us? Or is our biggest failure being 'out-of-touch', and our greatest need a closer daily walk with God? What are the marks of a Spirit-filled life?

8. *Should all speak in tongues?*

Paul's question at the end of 1 Corinthians 12 seems to most readers to be crying out for the answer 'No!', as in the case of each of the other questions he asks at that point. Yet some teach that speaking in tongues is the incontrovertible sign that we have had 'the baptism of the Spirit'. Is this an 'evangelical fantasy' or biblical realism? What does the Bible really say?

9. *Has Rome changed?*

Or have the apparently huge changes since Vatican II been more a matter of window-dressing? Those who represented the Church of England in the ARCIC talks seem confident that Rome has changed. Some leading evangelicals have been telling us that not only was the separation from Rome at the time of the great sixteenth-century Reformation a tragic mistake, but that it was due primarily to a simple misunderstanding on the part the Reformers of what Rome really taught, and on the part of the Roman Catholics of what the Reformers were saying. This makes me wonder whether those who are saying such things have ever read the decrees of the Council of Trent! Are Roman Catholics and Protestants really teaching the same things today in slightly different terminology? Or are some so-called Protestants fudging the issues in the interests of ecumenical unity?

10. Who is the church for?

Many are telling us, and rightly so, that one of the main reasons for the existence of Christ's church here on earth is to reach outsiders with the good news. Archbishop Temple's saying, 'The church is the only society which exists for the benefit of non-members' is often quoted. But is this the whole truth? What do the Scriptures say? Have we been too inward-looking? If so, how can we correct this?

11. Do all roads lead to God?

Although most evangelicals will be quite sure in their own minds that Christianity is unique, and is the only way to God, there may be some timid souls who are powerfully influenced by what highly trained professionals in high places say. They need help — not from contrary opinion, but from the Scriptures. We must bring everything to the bar of Scripture! I doubt if believers in Britain will get into trouble in the last decade of the twentieth century for declaring themselves to be Christians. That is one of many options in this permissive age! What may well bring persecution, probably from the more religious elements, could be declaring that Christ is the *only* way to the Father, or even failing to toe the line marked out by others who say, 'This ecumenical unity is God's will for all of us.' We need to be sure of our ground.

Recommended for further reading

Don Carson, *Showing the Spirit, An Exposition of 1 Corinthians 12-14*, Baker Book House.

Don Carson, *From Triumphalism to Maturity, 2 Corinthians 10-13*, IVP.

Philip Hughes, *2 Corinthians*, Zondervan.

Hywel Jones, *Gospel and Church, An evangelical evaluation of ecumenical documents on church unity*, Evangelical Press of Wales, 1989.

J. A. MacArthur, *The Charismatics*, Zondervan.

Victor Budgen, *The Charismatics and the Word of God*, Evangelical Press.

E. H. Andrews, *The Spirit has Come*, Evangelical Press.

Peter Masters, *The Healing Epidemic*, Tabernacle Bookroom

David Lewis, *Healing — Fantasy or Fact?* Hodder & Stoughton

Dr Nolan, *Doctor in search of a miracle*.

Dr Nolan joined Kathryn Kuhlman's team so as to observe at first hand.

Bernard Palmer, ed., *Medicine and the Bible*, Paternoster Press for Christian Medical Fellowship, 1986.

Vincent Edward & Gordon Scorer, *Some thoughts on Faith Healing*, Christian Medical Fellowship.

S. I. McMillen, *None of These Diseases*, Fleming Revell.

Dave Hunt & T. A. McMahon, *The Seduction of Christianity*, Harvest House, 1985.

Noel Weeks, *The Sufficiency of Scripture*, Banner of Truth Trust, 1988.
Francis Schaeffer, *The Great Evangelical Disaster*, Kingsway, 1985.
D. W. Bebington, *Evangelicalism in Modern Britain — A History from 1730-1980*, Unwin Hyman, 1989.
Reg Burrows, *Dare to Contend*, Jude Publications.
Walter Martin, *The New Age Cult*, Bethany House.

Index